The Case Writer's Toolkit

June Gwee

The Case Writer's Toolkit

June Gwee
Asian Business Case Centre, College of Business (Nanyang Business School)
Nanyang Technological University
Singapore

ISBN 978-981-10-7172-0   ISBN 978-981-10-7173-7   (eBook)
https://doi.org/10.1007/978-981-10-7173-7

Library of Congress Control Number: 2017959587

Cover image by Wendy Wong.

Printed on acid-free paper

This Palgrave Macmillan imprint is published by Springer Nature
The registered company is Springer Nature Singapore Pte Ltd.
The registered company address is: 152 Beach Road, #21-01/04 Gateway East, Singapore
189721, Singapore

For Dennis, Nathan and Joel

FOREWORD

I have witnessed the value of case studies first-hand. For more than two decades, I was involved with case studies—as case author, case teacher and case centre director. I wrote and taught case studies on business strategy, organisation transformation, innovation, urban development and public governance. Through these involvements, I discovered that case studies help develop systemic understanding and insights into why and how things are done. We learn how organisations, managers and leaders develop strategies and policies, implement them as well as adapt and change over time. These insights were instrumental in the development of my book *Dynamic Governance: Embedding Culture, Capabilities and Change in Singapore*.

It was during my research for this book that I met June and started out collaboration on developing and co-writing case studies. We worked together on several cases of the Singapore Public Service and when she was seconded to the Asian Business Case Centre (ABCC) of the Nanyang Business School at the Nanyang Technological University. June is a great case writer and has coached and mentored many younger case writers in the ABCC and the Civil Service College.

Through case studies, we can better analyse patterns of development over time. Every event or action occurs in a real-life, specific context. The benefits of learning through case studies are obvious. Students learn deeply through case discussions. Leaders and managers learn through interacting with case writers. Organisations better understand the rationale behind each path of success and failure. Case writers learn by studying organisations and individuals. Because case studies are anchored on real-life events and people, these narratives allow us to develop practice-based insights.

When we study organisations and individuals, we develop skills to identify issues and problems, think conceptually in different circumstances and
take action using practical intelligence. It is interesting to research into
how organisations and industries work and mine the tacit knowledge
which resides in people and organisations. Always, there are fascinating
insights and unexpected discoveries that either reinforce existing ideas or
question assumptions.

Because of these benefits of learning through cases, there is space to
develop more cases, especially in the Asian context. The case method and
early case studies originated from educators and researchers in North
America and Europe. Understandably, there are more case studies about
American and European organisations, written from western perspectives,
compared to case studies about Asian organisations written through Asian
eyes. Every day, there are many new and captivating Asian stories with
interesting lessons about people and organisations that remain untold.

We need more people to write case studies about their organisations,
industries and sectors, especially Asian-focused case studies. In 1999,
when I first became Dean of the Nanyang Business School, I founded the
Asian Business Case Centre which also became the first case centre in
Singapore. The Centre was funded by a donation from the late Lee Seng
Wee, a Singaporean philanthropist, banker and businessman who received
his MBA from the Western University of Canada. This resulted in a collaboration between the Nanyang Business School and the Ivey Business
School. Researchers and faculty from Nanyang and Ivey co-authored
many case studies which enabled Nanyang faculty to learn the craft of case
writing and Ivey researchers to learn about Asian businesses and
industries.

Over time, Asian case writers have become better in writing about Asian
experiences, organisations and contexts. However, it is still challenging to
ground the case study narrative on evidence and concepts in such a way
that it engages readers. A good case writer is a good researcher, writer,
educator, marketer and storyteller. Presenting and delivering content is as
important as developing content. The case writer is a keen observer, possesses sensibility and is motivated by curiosity about people, events and
organisations.

Case writing takes much skill and experience, which June has captured
from her experience researching and writing case studies, working with
others to develop case studies and teaching case writing. There are very

few professional research writers in the field who write case studies for a living which makes this book a rich and unique book by a practitioner.

Some of the common questions that amateur case writers ask are 'What is a case study?', 'How long is a case study?', 'What is the process of writing one?', 'How do I decide what to put in my case study?', 'What makes a case study engaging?', 'How do I structure my case study?'. The answers to these questions are found in this book. It contains step-by-step case development techniques and practical advice for writers to directly apply to their case study project. There are also explanations of theories and concepts behind the techniques.

I welcome the publication of this book and I encourage case writers and would-be case writers to read this book. I hope that more will be inspired to write case studies about their organisations, industries and communities.

Canon Professor of Business   Neo Boon Siong
Dean, College of Business (Nanyang Business School)
Director, Asian Business Case Centre
Nanyang Technological University
Singapore
29 May 2017

PREFACE

The writer's workshop is everywhere and anywhere. In the study, at the office, on the train, in the café, the list is endless. Wherever the workshop, the writer's toolkit is indispensable. Every writer's toolkit is unique. Some swear by pens and moleskin journals, others depend on their MacBooks, many have a style guide as loyal companion. These are the writer's physical instruments. But the writer also has other intangible tools—his/her five senses, passion, imagination, intuition, resilience, discipline, sensibility, attention to detail as well as the skill of making the intangible tangible— which is what this book is about. Using these tools, writers reveal insights about people and their worlds. Writing case studies is no different. Case writers narrate, describe and explain facts in an engaging and authentic manner, but with less drama and more pragmatic realism.

My first encounter with case studies was when I was studying for a Chartered Institute of Marketing qualification, and case studies were part of the written examination to qualify for the diploma. A lengthy and complex case study was given as pre-reading, while questions about the case were given on the day of the exam. To prepare for the exam, I attended classes on how to dissect and analyse case studies. These lessons taught me how to process a case study for examination. Later, I used case studies as a qualitative research method for my postgraduate studies where I studied key issues in nation branding and developed theoretical frameworks on strategic design management. Since then, I have been fascinated by the richness and varied uses of case studies for research, teaching, learning, transmitting knowledge and general reading.

When I used case studies as a student, I regarded them as a means to an end—to get the grades I need to graduate. With each case study, I would strip it apart, deconstruct it, examine it with a microscope. Later, when I chanced upon case studies again as a general reader and without the pressures of being assessed for my critical analysis, I realised that the styles and quality of case studies differed considerably. For some, I was engaged and read from beginning to end in a single sitting. With others, I could not move past the first page. I was most intrigued by case studies that had an insightful story with some unexpectedness but written in clear and simple language. Having read so many of them, most case studies faded away except those which moved me, gave me new perspectives or changed my mind about what I previously believed to be true. It was when I had to write case studies that I realised that developing a story idea and writing it into a case study took more effort than it looked.

As case writers, we need to be ambidextrous—to function superbly as a wordsmith and researcher, as well as to enter the psyche of readers to see how they would perceive the words and ideas that we write. Because case studies are real episodes of life based on facts told from a certain perspective, the case writers play god and decide on the perspective of how facts will be told and how they will be assembled to reveal events and issues within a specific time and space. These non-fiction documentaries are not figments of case writers' imagination, nor are they written for entertainment. It is the responsibility of case writers to ensure that case studies are accurate representations of the actual situation. If for various reasons case studies are disguised, this should be made known to the reader. Case writers are purposeful and accurate with their composition, yet making it look effortlessly put together for the reader. This is a skill that can be learnt, and this toolkit will explain how you can develop this skill.

Unique Features

There are many books on case writing. Some are academic, others are practical with many worksheets and exercises. Most are centred on the teaching case and the case method. I wanted this toolkit to extend the work of current experts by including information and material on case studies that are written for purposes other than the case method. This will help case writers and organisations use case studies for knowledge capture and to learn on their own.

The manuscript of this book was completed in 2016, but I spent some time refining the illustrations and examples in the book to make sure that their form best represents the concepts. All writers suffer from some sort of obsession with duality—light exists because of darkness, genius borders on madness, love battles hate. I am convinced that case writers are both tactile and visual learners. They learn best through both words and images. This is the reason why this book has visual aids such as illustrations, figures, tables and charts. I hope that these will help to simplify learning for new writers.

We learn to write by reading, observing, thinking, discussing, modelling good writing and getting feedback. You will find examples and frameworks to help you get started. These are based on my own experience of writing cases, teaching writing workshops and guiding case writers. In time, you will also customise some of these tools for your topic and purpose. At the end of the day, these tools are only as good as the craftman—the writer. More importantly, we learn to write by doing, so just keep on writing.

THE STRUCTURE OF THIS BOOK

This book is divided into six parts. Part I describes the function and purpose of case studies and how they came about. Chapter 1 informs the case writer about the toolkit and explains the richness of case studies. This first chapter defines the case study and explains the function of case studies. It gives an overview of the case universe, highlighting some of the similarities and differences of different case studies. I have focused on three genres of case studies in this book—the teaching case, research case and knowledge-capture case. There is a description of how each of these genres evolved, including some of their developments in Asia. Case studies are purpose-centric. The content, design, structure, format and presentation of a case study are dependent on how it is intended to be used. With this knowledge, case writers can then decide on what they want to do with their case studies.

Part II of the book contains three units which explain the process of case development. Chapter 2 describes the Writer's Compass. This is the tool that guides case writers on how to develop case studies. Just like a compass with equal but opposite magnetic poles, The Writer's Compass has three pairs of unique and opposite activities that keep the case study project in balance. These six poles are: identify angle, develop case concept plan, research and analyse, write, review and refine and publish and launch. Each of these six areas is explained in detail to give readers a good overview of the case development process.

Following the description of the Writer's Compass, Chap. 3 explains the Case Roundel—a tool to conceptualise and plan the case study. The Case Roundel is a circular window that helps case writers capture their perspective of the case study topic and approach. This is the writer's point of view of the story he/she wants to tell, what the case will be used for, who will use it, how will it be used, where will it be used, what is needed to produce it, what form will it take and how long will it take to develop it. Two important but often neglected aspects in developing a case concept—knowing your target reader and engaging your stakeholders—are also included in this chapter. At the end of the chapter, a case concept plan of an actual case study is provided for case writers to model and develop their own.

Chapter 4 of Part III guides case writers in conducting research for their topic. The Research Rhombus helps writers think about their project step-by-step. The purpose of this chapter is not to equip case writers with comprehensive skills in qualitative research but to give them sufficient knowledge and skill to collect information for writing their case studies. There are many good books on qualitative research methodology that case writers can consult on their own if they want to deepen their qualitative research skills. One of the significant strata of the Research Rhombus is analysis of the information collected. This chapter describes four methods to help case writers make sense of the data collected and develop insights for their case studies.

Part III focuses on the form of the case study. Form is the shape in which the case study should take. Amateur case writers instinctively look for a template to help structure their case studies. Although I do not believe that a writer's composition and creativity should be constrained by pre-cast templates, the Case Jigsaw in Chap. 5 is a tool for case writers to help them create a structure to hold together the contents of the case study. The Case Jigsaw comprises eight pieces that case writers can work on independently or together to consolidate their story. It helps case writers construct their case studies piece by piece, informed by the Case Roundel and Research Rhombus. Although this is a basic tool, it is up to case writers' imagination and creativity to bring their case studies to life. Form follows function, which is the reason for locating the Case Jigsaw in this chapter of the book. Case writers have to decide on the function of the case study before shaping it. To illustrate this, this chapter also contains specific examples related to the Case Jigsaw such as how to write the title, opening, context, characters, issues, incidents, tensions and closing.

Part IV discusses the case writer's craft. The Chronicler's Rune in Chap. 6 is a symbol comprising the letter 'C' for Chronicler, 'S' for Style, 'L' for Linguistics and 'V' for Voice because you cannot separate the storyteller from his craft. The chronicler is the storyteller whose writing style and voice are intermeshed with his choice and use of words. Just like craftsmen, the case writers' composition uses all these elements, as well as incorporating their experience and endless hours of practice. For amateur and non-native English writers, this chapter also explains basic grammar, syntax and semantics in layman terms. While linguistic skill can be learnt, writing style, voice and experience are forged through time. There is also a section on how to obtain permissions from stakeholders to release and publish case studies.

Part V contains examples of case studies to show how function, process, form and craft are combined in composition. Although all the case studies that are mentioned and cited in this book can be found online in case study repositories of institutions or in national libraries, I have written and adapted some of my research into case studies to highlight distinct features of common case studies. Chapter 7 has examples of a process case study, ethics case study, strategy case study and comparative study. There are also sections that explain what is a multimedia case study, and what makes a star case study. I have chosen to highlight these mainly because I had researched and analysed these categories over the past decade. However, this is only a small subset of the universe of case studies.

Chapter 8 of Part V advises case writers how to edit their own work. It is also a guide for editors and reviewers of case studies. Very often, case writers are so caught up with telling their story that they develop blind spots. The Editor's Rubric is a tool to help them step away from their work and see their writing wearing the hat of an editor or reviewer. With this in mind, writers, reviewers and editors can use the Editor's Rubric to check off each item and determine whether the case study that they are reading meets the requirements of a star case study.

Part VI is the final section of this book. It is centred on using case studies for teaching. Chapter 9 provides an overview of the key concepts and features of the case method in the context of case writing so that you can have a holistic view of case studies. The advantage of this chapter is that it is a good summary of the key features of the case method. It also contains examples of teaching plans which incorporate instructional design theories. This gives structure and theoretical framework to how a case method session can be framed and choreographed to achieve maximum learning outcome.

Chapter 10 lists the components of a teaching note and explains how you can write one for your teaching case. There is an example of a teaching note using an actual case study highlighted in the earlier chapters to demonstrate how lesson plan and case analysis are combined into a single document.

Through these 10 chapters, case writers can participate in the journey of a single strategy case study titled SingTel Yellow Pages—how it is developed from case concept in Chap. 3, to research and analysis in Chap. 4, shaped in Chap. 5, composed in Chap. 7 and supported by a teaching note in Chap. 10.

Singapore   June Gwee

ACKNOWLEDGEMENTS

This book is possible because I have been able to learn from many good teachers of case writing and the case method from the Harvard Business School, Harvard Kennedy School, Ivey Business School, IMD Business School and Evans School of Public Policy and Governance. They introduced me to their frameworks on writing case studies and were instrumental in helping me refine my own thinking and hone my skills in this area.

Special thanks to Professor Neo Boon Siong of the Nanyang Business School who has been my co-author for many case studies. He has generously shared his expertise and experience on case studies, always pushing boundaries and encouraging the development of insights for all the projects that we had worked on. I have been able to experiment on the form and function of case studies because of our collaboration.

To my peers and colleagues from the Asian Business Case Centre and the Nanyang Business School, especially Geraldine and Siew Kien who worked together with me to review case studies. A big thank you to the team and the faculty of the Nanyang Business School for the endless questions and discussions which pushed me to conceive new ways to clarify case studies, define quality and deepened my work in unravelling the mysteries of case writing and storytelling. I am glad to have joined this team.

This book would not have been possible if not for my peers and bosses, who had taken an interest in my work, supported my crazy ideas, egged me on to discover new paths and challenged me during different phases of my career. Wendy, so glad that you were part of my journey to brainstorm the images in this toolkit. It has been fun creating and watching the shapes tell their story. Most of all, to Dennis, Nathan and Joel who patiently tolerated and supported me during the madness of writing and publishing.

Last but not least, I'm always grateful to learners from diverse backgrounds who attended my case writing workshops and whom I've coached. You have continuously challenged me to explain the case writing process and techniques better, and in ways that are relevant to your context. I hope that this toolkit is the beginning of the adventure for you.

CONTENTS

About the Author

June Gwee is a Fellow at the Asian Business Case Centre of the Nanyang Business School in the Nanyang Technological University, Singapore, specialising in case studies, teaching case writing workshops and coaching case writers. She is also senior principal researcher at the Civil Service College, Singapore. Some of her previous publications include *Case Studies: Building Communities* (2015), *Case Studies in Public Governance: Building Institutions in Singapore* (2012) and *Art and Design for Strategic Management: Culture as Strategy* (2008).

Since 1993, she has been using case studies for research, training and knowledge capture. Her research interests are in the areas of strategy and innovation, art and design and narrative methods where she drew from her work experience in marketing communications, publications and content development. During her career in the private and public sectors, she had managed key projects in brand design, corporate communications and publishing.

June received her PhD in Visual Arts from the University of Sydney, Australia, for her research on art and design management. She has a Master of Science degree in International Marketing from the University of Strathclyde, United Kingdom, and a Bachelor of Arts degree with majors in English Literature and Economics from the University of Calgary, Canada. June has a Diploma in Adult and Continuing Education (DACE) and an Advanced Certificate in Training and Assessment (ACTA) from the

Institute of Adult Learning, Singapore. She also has a Diploma in Marketing from the Chartered Institute of Marketing, United Kingdom (CIM). She received a Public Administration Medal (Bronze) at the 2015 National Day Awards.

LIST OF FIGURES

LIST OF TABLES

PART I

Function

CHAPTER 1

Introduction

There is never just one path.

Telling real-life, non-fiction stories requires skill and craft which are the critical tools that case writers need to draw from their toolkit. The case writer's toolkit contains five tools to design and compose effective case studies. These are the Writer's Compass, Case Roundel, Research Rhombus, Case Jigsaw, and Chronicler's Rune. I've chosen geometric figures to depict each of these tools for two reasons. First, geometric figures are formed simply by a combination of lines and points on a single plane or space. There is technical precision, mathematical accuracy and conceptual balance in the formation of each geometric figure which symbolises the scientific aspect of a case writer's tool. At the same time, the geometric figures are versatile because they can be combined to form other geometric shapes. For example, by flattening a circle, you get an oval, and putting two isosceles triangles together, a quadrilateral is formed. This is the writer's creative craft—using imagination, knowledge and mastery of his/her tools to create an effective piece of work.

The circle, quadrilateral and triangle are the main geometric shapes in our world. By manipulating these three basic shapes, artists can sketch almost anything they see around them. Likewise for case writers, these three shapes are the building blocks of their toolkit for writing engaging and meaningful case studies. Hence, the case writer's toolkit is a kaleidoscope (Fig. 1.1) of the Writer's Compass, Case Roundel, Research Rhombus,

© The Author(s) 2018
J. Gwee, *The Case Writer's Toolkit*,
https://doi.org/10.1007/978-981-10-7173-7_1

Fig. 1.1   The case writer's toolkit

Case Jigsaw and Chronicler's Rune. The toolkit is dynamic, creative and alive, representing the writer's skill, craft and imagination to compose an engaging case study.

1.1   DEFINING THE CASE STUDY

Before we examine and use each of these tools, we need to answer a fundamental question—'what is a case study?'. This is an important question because to know how to write a case study, you must first understand its function.

The case study can serve different purposes. Depending on how you intend to use it, the case study can be defined in many ways (see Table 1.1).

Table 1.1 Case study definitions

Howard Husock (1997) in *An Outline for Casewriters and Case Teachers, Kennedy School of Government*	Robert K. Yin (1984) in *Case Study Research: Design and Methods*	Colorado State University
A teaching case is a story describing or based on actual events that justifies careful study and analysis by students. For example, of a crisis in foreign policy decision-making. Like any story, a case presents a conflict, typically the tension between alternative courses of action that bring different viewpoints, interests and values into contention and that must be resolved by a decision.[1]	A case study is an empirical inquiry that investigates a contemporary phenomenon within its real-life context, especially when the boundaries between phenomenon and context are not clearly evident. The case study inquiry copes with the technically distinctive situation in which there will be many more variables of interest than data points, and as one result relies on multiple sources of evidence, with data needing to converge in a triangulating fashion, and as another result benefits from the prior development of theoretical propositions to guide data collection and analysis.[2]	Case study refers to the collection and presentation of detailed information about a particular participant or small group, frequently including the accounts of subjects themselves. A form of qualitative descriptive research, the case study looks intensely at an individual or small participant pool, drawing conclusions only about that participant or group and only in that specific context.[3]
Rolf Johansson (2003) in *Case Study Methodology*	John S. Hammond (2009) in *Learning by the Case Method*	William Naumes and Margaret J. Naumes (2012) in *The Art & Craft of Case Writing*
A case is a phenomenon specific to time and space.[4]	Cases show actual problems and decisions that a company has faced.[7]	A case is a factual description of events that happened at some point in the past.[5]
Carnegie Mellon University	University of New South Wales	Merriam-Webster Dictionary
Case studies are stories. They present realistic, complex and contextually rich situations and often involve a dilemma, conflict, or problem that one or more of the characters in the case must negotiate.[6]	A case study is an account of an activity, event or problem that contains a real or hypothetical situation and includes the complexities you would encounter in the workplace. Case studies are used to help you see how the complexities of real life influence decisions.[10]	A published report about a person, group, or situation that has been studied over time. A situation in real life that can be looked at or studied to learn about something.[8]
Hong Kong University		Stanford University
Case study is a learning practice that shifts the emphasis from lecture-based activities to more student-based activities.[9]		In general terms, case studies can assess the applications of concepts to complex real-world situations, including building analytical skills that distinguish high priority from low priority elements.[11]

From these definitions, a case study can be a story, a report, a research method, a tool for teaching and an assessment method. For this toolkit, I will use this definition of a case study:

A case study is an objective account of real events in a complex environment where a person, organisation or country faces dilemmas and conflicts. The case study provides insights, challenges the thinking of readers and engages them to critically think or act on the issues discussed in the case study.

1.1.1   Case Vignettes and Case Scenarios

Case vignettes and case scenarios are variants of case studies. A case vignette can be based on a real or hypothetical situation, or an imagined future situation. In theatre and literature, a vignette refers to a short, impressionistic scene that describes a single moment or character, while a scenario refers to a collage of events, just like a scene in a play or a movie. If we borrow from these definitions, then a scenario can be explained as a compilation of vignettes. Compared to a scenario, a vignette would have less information and would be very specific. Vignettes are snapshots—brief, informal and quick descriptions—usually not more than a page. Because of their brevity, they seldom have depth, breadth and complexity of issues.

In medicine, social studies, psychology and ethics, case vignettes are written to help students interpret information, diagnose problems, recommend treatments and make decisions while confronted with a dilemma or conflict. Like case studies, vignettes and case scenarios are also used for teaching and developing thinking skills, communication skills, reasoning skills, decision-making skills and problem-solving skills.

1.2   Types of Case Studies

The case universe comprises three main types of case studies:

- The teaching case: a case study that is used for teaching, usually as part of the case method
- The research case: a case study that is used as a qualitative research method
- The knowledge-capture case: a case study that documents an event, issue or incident

The origins and evolution of these three main types of case studies are described in the following sections.

1.2.1 The Teaching Case

The case study made its first appearance as part of the case method in 1800s. Then, the case method was used to teach medicine, psychology, sociology and law.[12] The case method is a teaching approach where a skilled instructor facilitates discussion among learners based on a real-life, story-based scenario called the case study. Then, case studies were presented as a historical description of an event or incident where the actions were explained and the results of these actions were documented. This method of learning through dialogue and probing questions by the instructor is based on the Socratic method which is focused teaching through inquiry. This is different from the classic lecture method where the role of the instructor is to impart knowledge to students and the role of students is to receive knowledge from the instructor.

Inductive Teaching and Learning in North America
The case study is most commonly associated with Harvard University. In 1870, when Christopher Columbus Langdell, a student of the Harvard Law School,[13] became professor and dean of the Harvard Law School,[14] he favoured the inductive teaching and learning method and gave students case studies for them to analyse and draw their own conclusions. Students would first read law cases on their own to glean the basic principles of law, then attend class discussions on the cases that they had read.[15] In class, the instructor would interrogate the students on the facts of the case, underlying rules of law and reasons behind their arguments. Up until then, law had been taught using the Dwight method of instruction where students learnt through a combination of lecture, recitation and drill.[16] With the Socratic method, it trained students in critical thinking because the 'correctness' of answers was dependent on perspective which meant that there would be more than one 'correct' answer. Students were expected to collect their own evidences, apply critical analysis to formulate conclusions, and defend their judgement and decisions.

However, Harvard University was not the only university to use this method during that period. The Collége St-Joseph on Île Perrot in

Quebec, Canada, also used the Socratic method. Joseph Octave Maufette, founder of Collége St-Joseph, explained in the 1888 edition of his college calendar: 'Our education goal is not to stuff our pupils' heads with facts of doubtful utility that they will likely forget as soon as they come out of college, but rather to instill practical knowledge and, above all, to allow them to grow into the habit of logical and correct reasoning in every subject.'[17]

In 1920, when Wallace B. Donham, a graduate of the Harvard Law School, became dean of the Harvard Business School, he adopted the case method as the School's main method of instruction.[18] Students were given one case study per class and they would prepare using assignment questions that were provided together with the case. The focus of the case was on the difficult choice of the protagonist: 'What should he do?' Class participation during the case session comprised 50% of the grade.[19] By 1924, the case method became the main method in the School.[20] It was reported that under his leadership, 18,900 cases were written between 1920 and 1947.[21]

Bringing the Case Method and Case Studies Overseas
In 1919, Dr W. Sherwood Fox, Dean of Arts and Science, and Dr K. P. R Neville, Registrar, of the University of Western Ontario in London, Canada, began to use the Harvard case method to teach business.[22] By then, the Harvard Business School had started to establish 'outposts' for case studies by helping universities such as the University of Western Ontario to start their own business or management education programmes.[23] Andrew R. Towl led the Harvard Business School's case-related programmes and became a champion for the Harvard Business School case method when he joined the school in 1944.[24] Towl became Director of Case Development and Director of the Intercollegiate Case Clearing House, and was known as the leading authority on case method teaching and research.[25] He supervised the development of cases and their distribution within the Harvard Business School and to business schools around the world. He was known to have travelled to 37 countries to teach and explain the Harvard Business School case method.[26]

In the 1960s, Professor Michiel R. Leenders and Professor James Erskine engaged in research to re-engineer the case method.[27] They wrote and published *Case Research: The Case Writing Process* in 1973 which later morphed into the book *Writing Cases* when they were joined by co-author Louise A. Maufette-Leenders in 1978. A subsequent book titled *Teaching with Cases*, based on interviews with over 100 case teachers, was published in 1981.[28] These were among the earlier publications that articulated a theoretical framework behind case teaching and writing.

During the 1960s, the Medical School at McMaster University in Canada also developed a new form of learning called problem-based learning where cases were used as a trigger for self-study, before students were taught concepts and theories.[29] For this purpose, case studies were not intended to be receptacles of content. This method was based on cognitive science which found that learning and retention increased when there was motivation to learn.

Later, in 1985, the case method was used in the Harvard Medical School to help students and physicians assume responsibility for their own learning and stay current in their practice.[30] The School saw each medical encounter as a unique event with a specific patient at a specific point of time where medical students had to learn skills to respond and decide in such a situation. A case study had multiple parts which were revealed to the student progressively, imitating the doctor-patient encounter in the real world. As the story of the patient unfolded, students took responsibility for their own learning by making decisions regarding what they needed to know about the case.

The case method spread to Latin America during the late 1970s and early 1980s. The Brazilian Government signed a five-year contract with Professor Michiel R. Leenders to implant the case method at all universities that had a Master's programme in management or administration.[31] A Brazilian Case Clearing House was also established. As more educators were trained, the case method began to make its appearance in higher learning institutions in Argentina and Chili.[32]

The Case Method in Europe
In 1973, the Case Clearing House of Great Britain and Ireland was established.[33] When it first started, the clearing house was a joint initiative of 22 higher education institutions that wanted a channel to share case materials

among business teachers.[34] Many business schools in Europe had adopted the case method as a key method of instruction. More notably, the IE Business School in Spain, previously known as Instituto de Empresa, began to use the case method as a learning tool in the 1970s.[35] It was among the first few institutes in Europe to use case studies in pedagogy.[36]

With the popularity of the case method in Europe, the Case Clearing House was renamed the European Case Clearing House in 1991 to reflect the growth and reach of case teaching and case writing throughout Europe.[37] The European Case Clearing House was again renamed The Case Centre in 2013 to reflect the global scope of its business as a case distributor and knowledge platform of the case method.[38]

The Case Method in Asia

The case method began to be used in Chinese MBA programmes in 1974[39] following the introduction of MBA programmes in China. Then, MBA programmes were based largely on the western model. By 2001, it was reported that 3,054 China-context case studies were written and this formed 56% of MBA case studies used in 54 universities.[40]

In Hong Kong, the Asia Case Research Centre (ACRC) was set up as part of The University of Hong Kong in 1997 to develop teaching materials related to Asian businesses.[41] In Singapore, teaching cases were used at the Staff Training Insitute as early as 1974. In 2000, the Asian Business Case Centre (ABCC) was set up at the Nanyang Business School of Singapore's Nanyang Technological University to encourage the use and development of case studies on the Asian business experience.[42]

The case method became increasingly well-regarded as a good method of instruction to teach decision-making. When the Lee Kuan Yew School of Public Policy was established in August 2004, it adopted Harvard's approach in case development. Then, the School experimented with recruiting journalists and freelance feature writers to write case studies alongside the university's faculty. Journalists and feature writers were skilful in narrative writing techniques and helped package the intellectual content provided by professors into engaging and reader-friendly case studies. Faculty staff were paired with local writers, and they were trained by case method experts from leading institutions such as the Kennedy School of Government and the Evans School of Public Policy and Governance.

In August 2011, the Case Writing Initiative (CWI) was set up at the Centre for Management Practice in the Singapore Management University to promote case teaching and case writing.[43] The CWI produced Asian-based and international case studies to help students apply academic concepts in real-world situations. By 2015, CWI had developed more than 100 teaching cases and teaching notes.[44]

Multimedia Case Studies
Meanwhile, the Harvard Business School continued to innovate on the form of the teaching case and developed the first multimedia case study in 1996.[45] The case, 'Pacific Dunlop', contained interviews with protagonists and showed a tour of the production floor. This trend of developing multimedia or non-print cases continued into the 2000s. Harvard Business School launched the HBX, a course platform for online learning in 2015. Then, there were two main products within this platform—HBX videos featuring faculty and experts and HBX:Live which is a virtual classroom designed specifically for the case method. HBX Live allowed 60 international students to participate in a case discussion from their home county in real time, led by a Harvard professor.[46] The session was beamed live from a studio of the public broadcaster WBGH which was located outside of the University. The studio had 60 screens combined into a curved video wall; each screen displays the image of the 60 students. This was the first time that Harvard's traditional case method was conducted in a virtual classroom that imitated the delivery in a physical classroom.

Higher learning institutes in Europe were also incorporating technology into case studies and the case method. In 2017, IE Business School declared that it had a collection of 6000 teaching cases including 200 multimedia cases.[47] With the integration of technology and pedagogy, many universities and case publishers developed their own collection of print and online cases that incorporated both multimedia and simulation technologies. Case studies were chunked, delivered in segments and embedded with mini-documentaries or talking head interviews with protagonists.

The major distributors of teaching cases were, and still are, the Harvard Business School, Ivey Business School and The Case Centre. However today, business schools all over the world are also distributing their own case studies.

1.2.2   The Research Case Study

Although case studies were first made famous by universities, they were also used outside of the classroom as a research method, particularly in fields such as education and psychology. [48] In earlier years, they were often referred to as case works.[49]

A research case is part of a research method used to analyse a specific situation or issues for generating hypothesis or developing theoretical propositions. As part of research inquiry, case studies can be examined singly, for its own sake, or examined collectively to study patterns from various data points. Research cases can be used for comparative analysis of organisations, countries or even leadership styles of individuals. When used as research strategy, Yin (2009) had categorised case studies into different types; some of which can be used for knowledge-capture and teaching (explanatory cases, descriptive cases and interpretive cases), while others (exploratory cases and evaluative cases) are used more specifically for research.[50]

Types of Research Cases

In the 1970s, social scientist Robert Yin used the case study as a qualitative research method for social sciences. He identified three categories of case studies: exploratory, descriptive and explanatory.[51] Exploratory case studies explore phenomenon in the data (e.g. Does a student use any strategies in reading?). Descriptive case studies describe the phenomenon which occurs in the data (e.g. What are the different reading strategies and how they are used?). Explanatory case studies explain the phenomenon in the data (e.g. Why does a student use inferencing strategy during reading?). Since then, Yin's landmark publication on case study research[52] had been the authority on this topic.

In the 1990s, case study as a research method progressed. Case studies were used to teach nurses the nursing process. In nursing, case studies were used to study an individual, a family, an organisation or a place. Carla Mariano designed research studies based on either a single case or a multiple case.[53] A single case study investigates a single issue in a single situation. A single case study could involve an in-depth longitudinal study of an event or issue. On the other hand, a multiple case study examines the same issue in different situations or a specific situation from different perspectives.

In addition to these categories, McDonough and McDonough (1997) came up with two other categories of case studies: interpretive case studies and evaluative case studies.[54] Interpretive case studies interpret and evaluate data by developing conceptual categories to support or challenge assumptions made regarding them. Evaluative case studies make judgements about the phenomenon found in the data.

1.2.3   The Knowledge-Capture Case Study

Besides the case method and research, case studies are used for knowledge-capture, record-keeping and general reading. The purpose of knowledge-capture is to convey knowledge and encourage self-directed learning. Informed by research, all the facts are presented in the case study to enable readers to make their own analysis of the situation. These 'reading' cases are often stored in an organisation's knowledge management depository, or published. Their greater value is when readers gain deeper understanding and insights into events and decisions. Reading cases can be sub-divided into explanatory, descriptive and interpretive cases.

In Singapore, when the Institute of Policy Development was set up in 1993, Singapore-based case studies were used in the training of public officers. These case studies were written to document the policy rationales, dilemmas, lessons, successes and failures of Singapore's experience in public governance. They were used in classroom-based programmes where learners discussed the issues presented in the case studies. Through this method of learning, it was hoped that public officers, policymakers and students of public policy and administration could develop insights, question assumptions, acquire critical thinking and decision-making skills, and be inspired to improve policy and practice.

The Singapore public sector started a major documentation effort in 2009 to encourage public agencies to capture their institutional histories in the form of case studies. A documentation committee was set up within the Ministry of National Development to encourage its statutory boards to capture the policy rationales, processes and lessons of Singapore's development. Later, other public agencies also started documenting their own experience and used these case studies for internal training. These agencies saw value in collecting and curating the tacit knowledge of their retiring veterans in the form of case studies, to capture and transmit their organisation's experience, knowledge and culture, to train new generations of public officers.

The Civil Service College, a statutory board that was formed in 2001 and which subsumed the Institute of Policy Development, continued to use case studies for knowledge-capture, training and conducting discussions on policy development, ethics and values, institutional philosophies, principles of governance, leadership challenges, organisational transformations and public governance. Since 2009, the College had conducted many workshops to train public officers to develop case studies for their organisations.

1.3   CORE COMPONENTS OF A CASE STUDY

The case study is a descriptive account based on official documents, interviews, images and so on about people and events, their successes and failures, in the context of their environment. Although the purpose and use of case studies differ, these elements remain the same:

a. Contains a narrative

A case study tells a story of a person or institution facing a complex situation or dilemma. It identifies a problem, describes the issues within a context and contains a sequence of events. Embedded within the story are the cause and effect, plot, characters, relationships, points of view, setting, time, complexities, dilemmas, and challenges. Using an appropriate style and structure, the narrative moves the reader from one state (e.g. point of unknown) to another (e.g. a point of realisation) and reveals the consequences of actions, moral lessons and realities about the complexities of life.

b. Is based on real events and facts

A case study is a description or explanation of real persons and situations, based on actual facts, and not fiction. Case studies can be written from published information which makes it a secondary-source case, or it can be written based on field research, otherwise known as a primary-source case. This must be made known to the reader at the start of the case study. If the information has to be disguised because of confidentiality or non-disclosure requirements, this should be highlighted to the reader.

c. Contains insights

The purpose of a case study is enable readers to develop insights from stories. Learning occurs through several ways:

- use the story to transmit information and knowledge,
- use the story as a tool for readers to participate in active learning and develop new skills, or
- use the story to question assumptions and develop new thinking.

d. Is set within a specific space

The story within the case study is always set within a specific geographical and cultural space. This defines the physical and cultural boundary for the events and issues described in the case study. It helps the readers understand the context of where things happen, what are the values and beliefs of the community within this setting, the prevailing attitudes, and the way people think and behave within this setting.

e. Has a defined timeline

Case studies have a definite start and end point in time, that is, where do we choose to cut the story. The cut refers to the case writer's decision of where to start and end the story, as well as how to segment the story into logical parts in the body of the case study. The cut is selected based on the purpose, the subject matter and the angle of the case study. This is highlighted in the content of the case study so that readers are clear about when the story begins and ends. As case studies are based on real-life events which have a longer and larger continuum than what can be captured for the purpose of a case study, the specific cuts provide the time-frame for the story.

f. Has a protagonist

For a teaching case, the case narrative is often centred around a main character faced with difficult decisions. This main character is sometimes called the protagonist or the hero of the story. The protagonist is the lead character who is confronted with problems and dilemmas and has to find the best alternatives, solutions and decisions for these issues.

The benefit of incorporating a protagonist into the case narrative is that it helps to put readers in the shoes of the person and immerse themselves in the predicament faced by the person. It is possible to write case studies based on an organisation, committee or country, instead of a person. The only weakness in these types of narratives is that it distances the reader from the problem because there is no single person for the reader to identify with.

1.4   Using Case Studies

Case studies can be written on any subject. If you browse through the list of case studies distributed by case study publishers and university publishers, you will discover that they cover almost every major subject taught in higher education institutions.

Case studies are used for different purposes and they can be used in many ways. For example, Lundberg et. al. (2001) outlined nine types of cases: iceberg cases, incident cases, illustrative cases, head cases, dialogue cases, application cases, data cases, issue cases and prediction cases.[55] The intent of this book is to introduce first-time case writers to case studies, so I have simplified the categorisation of case studies to help new case writers working on their first case studies (Table 1.2).

Even with this simplified categorisation, you will notice that case studies often overlap in terms of use and function. An explanatory case is also a descriptive case but not all descriptive cases are necessarily explanatory. An illustrative case can be used for teaching, knowledge-capture or even research if it contains specific information that serves the purpose of research. Some cases are embedded with multiple issues, while others are straightforward but contain a difficult dilemma (Fig. 1.2).

Table 1.2 Types of case studies

Types of case studies	Description
Facilitated learning	
Decision case	A decision case puts readers in the shoes of a person, organisation, committee or country. Most widely used as a teaching case, the 'protagonist' in the decision case is presented with a series of options or alternatives and is forced to make a choice. It asks the basic question 'what should he/she do?' With each option, the protagonist faces dilemmas and trade-offs.
	There are often no right or wrong answers but a series of consequences for each decision. Students are made to ponder the protagonist's rationale and question the assumptions of each decision. Case studies that explore ethical dilemmas are largely decision cases. For example, how does a medical professional who is both a doctor and a religious leader in his community deal with end of life issues?
Application case	An application case describes the challenges and complexities of day-to-day management, operations, administration and the tactical implementation of strategies. In these areas, students can learn how to effectively implement strategies and plans using prescribed tools or approaches. The application case can range from applying financial valuation analysis, developing negotiation skills, conducting a cost benefit analysis to applying a market penetration strategy.
Research method	
Exploratory case	An exploratory case study investigates situations or problems that have no defined preliminary research. The purpose of exploratory cases is to establish priorities and definitions, improve research design, determine research strategy and method, and acquire insights to decide if more precise research should be conducted. Exploratory case studies provide initial research to discover patterns in data that can inform future research.

(*continued*)

Table 1.2 (continued)

Types of case studies	Description
Descriptive case	A descriptive case is a factual report of a single event or multiple events over a span of time. It documents how events occurred.
	They can describe organisational transformations, change management, institution-building, innovation, policy-making, public governance, strategic plans, corporate governance and cultural shifts. These issues are among the more complex and challenging for individuals, organisations, industries and nations because multiple issues and stakeholders are involved. The back and forth of decisions are deliberately captured to highlight the complexities of decision-making or implementation. For example, why is it difficult to change a nation's notion of success or how should the CEO transform a 50-year-old organisation?
	Descriptive case studies trace events over a longer timeframe because the impact of actions—whether the success or failures of strategies, policies, organisations, industries, institutions, societies and nations—are only seen over time. Hence, there is a tendency for descriptive case studies to be longer.
	Descriptive cases can be used as teaching cases although the length of these case studies may pose a challenge to both learners and instructors.
Explanatory case	An explanatory case explains and analyses the causes and effects of specific programmes or situations so as to understand what happened and the reasons that led to the outcome of the situation. Answering the question of 'why did things go wrong?', the explanatory case also captures the tacit knowledge of key actors and players, offering considerable insights from the data sources themselves.
	This genre of case studies can be used to explain strategies, processes and procedures. On one level, readers learn about the different phases of a project or the sequence of activities and events. At a deeper level, readers discover the thinking behind the strategies, process or framework, as well as the continual improvements or reviews needed. Explaining the origins and rationales of strategies and processes reduces the mechanistic nature of procedures and puts them in the context of a larger system.
Interpretive case	An interpretive case study describes a situation from a subjective point of view of the participant rather than as an objective observer of the situation. The emphasis in an interpretive case is not the reporting of facts but the researcher's interpretation of other people's perspectives. The purpose of an interpretive case study is to generalise findings.

(*continued*)

Table 1.2   (continued)

Types of case studies	Description
Evaluative case	An evaluative case study contains detailed information and assessments of specific situations for readers to judge these situations for themselves.
<u>Self-directed learning</u>	
Descriptive case	As indicated above
Explanatory case	As indicated above
Illustrative case	An illustrative case uses the description of a single event to illustrate, support or challenge theories, concepts, frameworks or assumptions. It describes specific situations or incidents and is generally quite brief. A vignette is an example of a small illustrative case. Best practice and failure cases are illustrative cases. Illustrative cases are also descriptive. They can be used for teaching, knowledge-capture and research.

All case studies, regardless of their categories, tell stories of people, organisations, industries and communities, set within specific contexts. The challenges and issues described in every story vary depending on the environment in which the story is based. Within the specific contexts in which the action unfolds, case study topics are wide-ranging:

- Culture—the ideas, customs, social norms, lifestyle and behaviour of a group of people.
- Ethics and values—the moral principles and code of conduct that direct people's behaviour.
- Innovation—new ways of work or way of life that change the behaviour of people, industry and society.
- Leadership—the ability and style of a person's action in achieving specific outcomes.
- Public governance and institutions—the process of governing, including the rules, norms, constructs of authority that influence the order, structure and behaviour of a society.
- Strategy and management—the plan of action and the administration of an organisation, a business or a function.
- Systems and structures—the procedures, approaches, framework and modus operandi of an entity.
- Technology—human inventions that change the way of life either through the use of machines, artificial intelligence or other non-human devices.

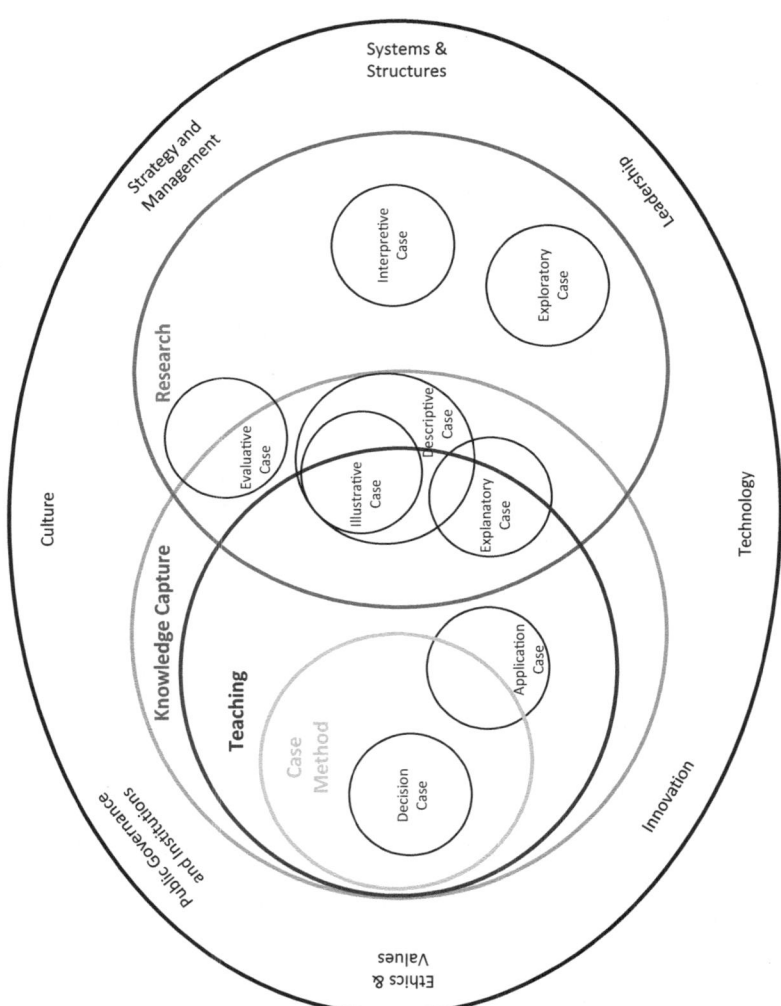

Fig. 1.2 The case universe

The list is endless. Visit the websites of any case publishers and you will see that there is an abundance of case studies written on business management, leadership, public administration, ethics, law, healthcare and so on. Over time, the function and form of case studies evolve and expand, making them complex and rich.

1.5   TRENDS AND LIMITATIONS

Despite the long tradition of case method in universities and adult education, there are those who question the efficacy of the case method and case studies as tools for developing industry-relevant skills and acumen.

a. Effective Peer Learning

The case method is a highly choreographed discussion method where students learn from peers and are led by a facilitator (see Chap. 9). To achieve this, peers and the instructor must have significant prior experience themselves to learn effectively from one another through the discussion. The lack of deep expertise, industry knowledge or work experience greatly limits deeper levels of professional learning. Case method should only be used as one of the many ways of instruction and not the only method of instruction.[56]

b. Suitability

Case method may not be the most suitable approach to teach statistics, physics and similar scientific and quantitative subjects where there are unique correct answers. These subjects may be better taught through other forms of instruction such as lectures, simulations or even through gamification.[57]

c. Generalisations

Case method requires students to make generalisations based on a set of given information found in the case study with no firm conclusions because there are no right and wrong answers. On its own, the method enable learners to develop critical thinking skills but does not equip learners with the tools and concepts and knowledge required of a specific discipline.[58] Neither does it teach learners 'how to separate historical fashions from universal principles—to distinguish unique events from the constant and timeless in human action.'[59]

d. Live Cases

The trend in business and executive education had been shifting to collaborative learning, that is, working in teams to solve real management problems faced by companies. This way, learners apply concepts and theories directly to problems and gain experience hands-on.[60] At Tippie's College of Business, University of Iowa, students were given experiential learning projects called 'live cases' where students work on real, immediate problems presented by the university's corporate partners, nonprofits and alumni. Students working on the projects speak to real customers, sales representatives and executives to take in their views when developing a strategy for the company.[61]

e. Limited Lifespan

Field-based case studies have a limited lifespan. A considerable amount of time is needed to conduct interviews, analyse, write them up and obtain release for use. While this is being done, the external environment is evolving rapidly and industries are constantly being disrupted. By the time the case study is ready for use, the issues described in the case may have lost their pertinence and currency, and hence are not as useful to readers and learners as when the case writer first started on it.

f. Resources

Case development is an expensive activity. To constantly develop new case studies, skilled case writers and strong subject matter experts are needed but they are not easily available. There is also an opportunity cost for these case writers who could otherwise pursue an academic career or provide consultancy services in their respective fields.

g. Research Rigour

On the research front, social science researchers have pointed out that there are limitations to using case studies as a research method. First, like all other research methods, case study research can be influenced by researcher bias. Second, the small sampling size could make it inaccurate or difficult to generalise findings and conclude from a single case. Third, case studies research is time-consuming and produces a large amount of data. The researcher would require considerable skill and discipline to manage and analyse the vast amount of data systematically.[62]

h. Case Study Length

Another trend is the growing demand for shorter case studies. Particularly, educators and students have been requesting for shorter and more compact cases, roughly two to three pages. A typical business teaching case normally comprised 10 to 20 pages of text and 5 to 10 additional pages of exhibits[63] where there is sufficient information for students to immerse themselves in the shoes of the main character, analyse the situation, make the best possible choices based on what they know from the case study and explain their decision.

Case studies that are used for research and knowledge-capture can be of varying lengths. They tend to be longer as they are used outside the classroom for in-depth reading and analysis. These could range from 10 to 60 pages, or more.

i. Declining Attention Span

Effects of the Internet, social media and a highly digital environment have changed the way people process information. Research has shown that readers now spend more time browsing, scanning and keyword spotting. They also demonstrate selective reading, non-linear reading and one-time reading. Less time is spent reading in-depth.[64] Other studies have also shown that expert video game players demonstrate higher levels of visual sensitivity.[65]

As the average human attention span falls, it has become more and more difficult for readers to go through 10 to 20 pages of text. If used in a programme, a teaching case is competing for the students' attention alongside other assigned readings.

In a consumer insights research study by Microsoft Canada, it was found that the average human attention span had declined from 12 seconds in 2000 to 8 seconds in 2013, and 9 seconds in 2014.[66] The research found that long-term focus declines with increased digital consumption and social media usage.[67] People who are heavy users of social media also tend to demonstrate high attention span but for short durations.[68] To deal with the decline in attention span, visual narratives (as well as text-based ones) should be guided by these principles:[69]

- To sustain attention, be clear, personal and to the point.
- To tackle selective attention and grab attention away from other stimuli, defy expectations, keep the message simple and keep things moving.
- To target alternating attention, embed calls to action, introduce interactivity, sequence messages, and continue experience through other touchpoints such as another screen or platform.

However, there are challenges in developing short cases. First, it is often difficult to capture the complexities of a real situation and its context within two to three pages while still delivering a rich account of a true story. Second, some issues and situations lend themselves well to short cases while others do not. It depends on the topic and purpose of the case study. Third, if one of the goals of case studies is to develop insights or learn decision-making skills, having short, compact cases may not be sufficient to develop skills in reading, information processing and critical thinking. Fourth, it takes as much skill, if not more, to write a short case study well.

Despite these limitations and criticisms, the case study is still a well-used device for learning about events, people, incidents and actions. As with any tool or method of instruction, it should serve a purpose while keeping to the principles of fairness, reliability, relevance and validity.

j. A Good Case Writer

There is a short supply of experienced case writers, largely because developing a good case study demands specific skills that are found across a range of occupations. Ideally, a good case writer has:

- qualitative research skills,
- analytical skills,
- aptitude for the development of insights,
- capacity to identify critical issues,
- ability to see the forest for the trees,
- skill to integrate theory with practice,
- strong command of the written and spoken language,
- originality in thinking and expressing ideas,
- ability to package and customise content to suit different types of target audience,
- relationship management skills,
- tolerance for ambiguity, and
- project management skills

NOTES

1. Husock, Howard (1997). "An Outline for Casewriters and Case Teachers". Cambridge, MA: Kennedy School of Government.
2. Yin, R. K. (2009). *Case study research: Design and methods.* 4th edition. Thousand Oaks, CA: Sage.
3. Colorado State University, Writing@CSU: The Writing Studio, "Case Studies". Retrieved on October 10, 2016 from http://writing.colostate.edu/guides/guide.cfm?guideid=60.
4. Johansson, Rolf (2003), "Case Study Methodology", Keynote speech at the International Conference *Methodologies in Housing Research* organized by the Royal Institute of Technology in cooperation with the International Association of People-Environment Studies, Stockholm, 22–23 September 2003. Retrieved on October 10, 2016 from http://psyking.net/HTMLobj-3839/Case_Study_Methodology-_Rolf_Johansson_ver_2.pdf.
5. Naumes William and Naumes Margaret J. Naumes (2012), *The Art & Craft of Case Writing*, Third Edition, New York: M.E. Sharpe, Inc.
6. Eberly Center: Teaching Excellence and Educational Innovation, Carnegie Mellon University. "Case Studies". Retrieved on October 7, 2016 from https://www.cmu.edu/teaching/designteach/teach/instructionalstrategies/casestudies.html.
7. Hammond, John S. (2009). "Learning by the Case Method". Boston, MA: Harvard Business Publishing. Retrieved on October 7, 2016 from https://cb.hbsp.harvard.edu/resources/marketing/docs/LearnCase_Mthd_M70235.pdf.
8. Merriam-Webster Dictionary. Retrieved on October 7, 2016 from http://www.merriam-webster.com/dictionary/case%20study.
9. Centre for Enhancement of Teaching and Learning, Hong Kong University. "Types of Assessment Methods", AR@HKU. Retrieved on October 7, 2016 from http://ar.cetl.hku.hk/am_case_study.htm.
10. UNSW Australia. "What is a Case Study?". Retrieved on October 7, 2016 from https://student.unsw.edu.au/what-case-study.
11. Center for Teaching and Learning, Stanford University. "Teaching with Case Studies", *Stanford University Newsletter on Teaching*, Winter 1994, Vol. 5, No. 2. Retrieved on October 7, 2016 from https://web.stanford.edu/dept/CTL/Newsletter/case_studies.pdf.
12. Naumes William and Naumes Margaret J. Naumes (2012), *The Art & Craft of Case Writing*, Third Edition, New York: M.E. Sharpe, Inc. Pg. 4.
13. Garvin, D. A. (2003). "Making the Case", *Harvard Magazine*, September-October 2003, Volume 106, Number 1.
14. Ibid.
15. Barton, B.H. (2008). "A Tale of Two Case Methods", *Tennessee Law Review*, Vol. 75, No. 3, University of Tennessee Legal Studies Research Paper No. 16.

16. Garvin, David A. (2003). "Making the Case". *Harvard Magazine*, September – October 2003, Volume 106, Number 1.
17. Leenders, M.R., Maufette-Leenders, L. A. and Erskine, J. A. (1973, 1978, 1989, 2001). *Learning with Cases.* London: Richard Ivey School of Business, The University of Western Ontario. p.v.
18. Gill, T.G. (2011). *Information with the Case Method: A Guide to Case Method Research, Writing, & Facilitation.* California, USA: Informing Science Press.
19. Garvin, David A. (2003). "Making the Case". *Harvard Magazine*, September – October 2003, Volume 106, Number 1.
20. Ewing, D. W. (1990). *Inside the Harvard Business School: Strategies and Lessons of America's Leading School of Business.* Crown, first edition.
21. "Harvard Business School and a Short History of the Case Method", https://globaleduc.wordpress.com/2013/09/10/the-harvard-business-school-and-the-case-study-method-like-a-horse-and-carriage/ (accessed on 5 Apr 2017).
22. Leenders, M.R., Maufette-Leenders, L. A. and Erskine, J. A. (1973, 1978, 1989, 2001). *Writing Cases.* London: Richard Ivey School of Business, The University of Western Ontario.
23. Based on email correspondence dated 2 May 2017 with Louise A. Maufette.
24. Andrew R. Towl Papers. HBS Archives. Baker Library Historical Collections. Harvard Business School. http://oasis.lib.harvard.edu/oasis/deliver/~bak00152, accessed on May 2, 2017.
25. Andrew R. Towl Papers. HBS Archives. Baker Library Historical Collections. Harvard Business School. http://oasis.lib.harvard.edu/oasis/deliver/~bak00152, accessed on May 2, 2017.
26. Marquard, Bryan. (July 15, 2012). Andrew R. Towl, 101, Harvard Business School Innovator. *The Boston Globe.* https://www.bostonglobe.com/metro/obituaries/2012/07/14/andrew-towl-was-director-case-development-harvard-business-school/WmE7ya3cg2q2U8F1jQ5IeJ/story.html. Accessed on May 2, 2017.
27. Based on email correspondence dated 2 May 2017 with Louise A. Maufette.
28. Ibid.
29. Garvin, David A. (2003). "Making the Case". *Harvard Magazine*, September – October 2003, Volume 106, Number 1.
30. Garvin, David A. (2003). "Making the Case". *Harvard Magazine*, September – October 2003, Volume 106, Number 1.
31. Based on email correspondence dated 2 May 2017 with Louise A. Maufette.
32. Ibid.
33. The Case Centre. *Our History.* https://www.thecasecentre.org/students/aboutus/organisation/history, accessed on May 2, 2017.
34. Ibid.
35. The Case Centre, *IE Business School.* http://www.thecasecentre.org/educators/ordering/whatsavailable/collections/iebussch, accessed on April 7, 2017.

36. The Case Centre, *IE Business School.* http://www.thecasecentre.org/educators/ordering/whatsavailable/collections/iebussch, accessed on April 7, 2017.
37. The Case Centre. *Our History.* https://www.thecasecentre.org/students/aboutus/organisation/history, accessed on May 2, 2017.
38. Ibid.
39. Hatch, James E. and Mu, Fengli (2015). *Use of the Case Method in Chinese MBA Programs.* Indiana, USA: Archway Publishing.
40. ibid.
41. The University of Hong Kong, *About ACRC,* http://www.acrc.hku.hk/about/about_cabc.asp, accessed on April 9, 2017.
42. Nanyang Technological University, *The Asian Business Case Centre,* http://www.nbs.ntu.edu.sg/Research/ResearchCentres/AsiaCase/Pages/default.aspx/, accessed on April 9, 2017.
43. Singapore Management University, *Case Writing Initiative,* accessed on January 9, 2017 from http://casewriting.smu.edu.sg/about-us.
44. Ibid.
45. Garvin, David A. (2003). "Making the Case". *Harvard Magazine,* September – October 2003, Volume 106, Number 1.
46. Harvard Business School, "HBX Launches HBX Live – Harvard Business School's Virtual Classroom", press release, 25 August 2015, http://www.hbs.edu/news/releases/Pages/hbx-live.aspx, accessed on April 9, 2017.
47. The Case Centre, *IE Business School,* accessed on January 10, 2017 from http://www.thecasecentre.org/educators/ordering/whatsavailable/collections/iebussch.
48. Starman, Adrijana Biba, "The case study as a type of qualitative research", *Journal of Contemporary Educational Studies 1/2013.* Retrieved on October 10, 2016 from http://www.sodobna-pedagogika.net/wp-content/uploads/2013/03/Starman1.pdf.
49. Merriam, S. B. (1988). *Case study research in education.* San Francisco, London: Jossey-Bass Publishers.
50. Yin, R.K., (2009). *Case Study Research: Design and Methods.* Fourth edition. Thousand Oaks, CA: Sage Publications.
51. Yin, R.K., (2009). *Case Study Research: Design and Methods.* 4th edition. Thousand Oaks, CA: Sage Publications.
52. Yin, Robert K., and Karen A. Heald 1975 "Using the case survey method to analyze policy studies." *Administrative Science Quarterly,* 20: 371–381; Yin, Robert K., Eveleen Bingham, and Karen A. Heald, 1976 "The difference that quality makes: The case of literature reviews." *Sociological Methods and Research,* 5: 139–156. Yin, Robert K., and Ingrid Heinsohn 1980. *Case Studies in Research Utilization." Washington: American Institutes for Research.*
53. Mariano, Carla (1995). The qualitative research process. In L.A. Talbot (Ed.), Principles and practice of nursing research (pp. 463–491). St. Louis,

MO: Mosby. Retrieved on October 10, 2016 from http://www.redorbit. com/news/science/130594/case_and_grounded_theory_as_qualitative_ research_methods/#9vvy1jkXvsCUMsqe.99.

54. McDonough, J. and McDonough, S., (1997). *Research Methods for English Language Teachers*. London: Arnold.

55. Lundberg, C. C. Rainsford, P., Shay, J., & Young, C. A. (2001) "Case writing reconsidered". Journal of Management Education, 25(4): 450–463.

56. Mitnick, Barry, "The Case Against the Case Method", *Harvard Business Review*, April 29, 2009, accessed on January 23, 2017 from https://hbr. org/2009/04/the-case-against-the-case-meth-1.

57. Yeaple, Ronald, "Is the MBA Case Method Passé?", *Forbes*, July 9, 2012, accessed on January 23, 2017 from http://www.forbes.com/sites/ronaldyeaple/2012/07/09/is-the-mba-case-method-passe/#f0eba4f31459.

58. Daniels, Mechan, "Why HBS Developed the Case Method – and What It's Like Today", *The Knewton* Blog, accessed on January 23, 2017 from https://www.knewton.com/resources/blog/test-prep/ why-harvard-developed-the-case-method-and-what-its-like-today/.

59. Kirkpatrick, Jerry, "Why Case Method Teaching Does Not Make Good History", accessed on January 23, 2017 from https://www.cpp. edu/~jkirkpatrick/Papers/CaseHist.pdf.

60. Yeaple, Ronald, "Is the MBA Case Method Passé?", *Forbes*, July 9, 2012, accessed on January 23, 2017 from http://www.forbes.com/sites/ronaldyeaple/2012/07/09/is-the-mba-case-method-passe/#f0eba4f3145.

61. Simons, John, "Business Schools Tackle 'Messy' Real-Time Corporate Issues', *The Wall Street Journal*, accessed on January 23, 2017 from http://www.wsj.com/articles/business-schools-tackle-messy-real-time-corporate-issues-1478102923.

62. Yin, R.K., (1984). *Case Study Research: Design and Methods*. Beverly Hills, Calif: Sage Publications.

63. Garvin, D. A. (2003). "Making the Case", *Harvard Magazine*, September-October 2003, Volume 106, Number 1.

64. Ziming Liu, "Reading behavior in the digital environment: Changes in reading behavior over the past ten years", Journal of Documentation, Vol. 61 Iss: 6, pp.700–712.

65. Boot WR, Kramer AF, Simons DJ, Fabiani M, Gratton G. "The effects of video game playing on attention, memory, and executive control." *Acta Psychol (Amst)*. 2008 Nov;129(3):387–98. doi:10.1016/j. actpsy.2008.09.005. Epub 2008 Oct 16.

66. Microsoft Canada, Consumer Insights (Spring 2015), *Attention Spans,* https://advertising.microsoft.com/en/wwdocs/user/display/cl/ researchreport/31966/en/microsoft-attention-spans-research-report.pdf.

67. Ibid.

68. Ibid.

69. Ibid.

PART II

Process

CHAPTER 2

The Writer's Compass

Every good journey needs a reliable guide.

Case writers are explorers. They hunt for case study ideas and story angles, examine evidence-based information and analyse masses of data to craft compelling content. The Writer's Compass is a tool to guide case writers through the six essential areas of the case writing journey (see Figure 2.1). It has six poles, instead of the four magnetic poles of a traditional compass, because the true north of a case study depends on the purpose of your case study, target readers, stakeholders, rules of engagement, and principles of good research. These vary over time, from project to project, place to place.

Like the poles of a compass, each area is an important and unique aspect of the case development process. When you follow through each of these areas sequentially, you will be able to produce your case study in an orderly and structured manner. *Identify Idea and Angle* is a mirror image of *Write* because it will be impossible to write the case study if the idea and angle are not clearly thought through. Likewise, *Develop Case Concept Plan* is an important reference point during *Review and Refine* because you need to check the final draft against the original intent of the case study. Finally, a case study is considered good for *Publication and Launch* only if its content is anchored in rigorous *Research and Analysis*.

© The Author(s) 2018
J. Gwee, *The Case Writer's Toolkit,*
https://doi.org/10.1007/978-981-10-7173-7_2

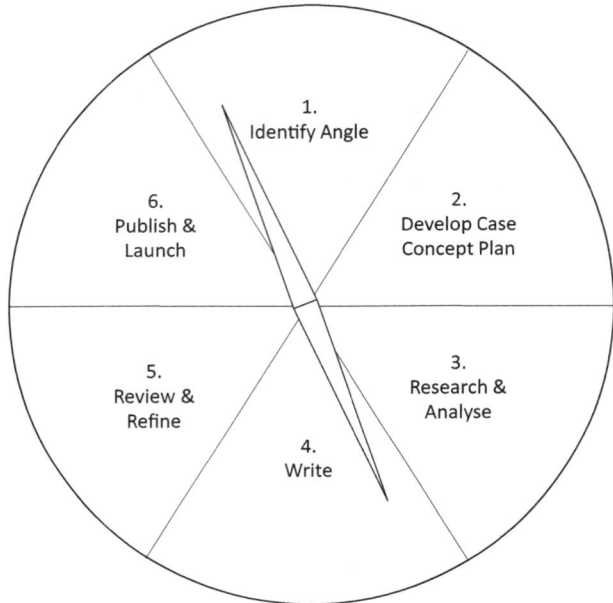

Fig. 2.1 The Writer's Compass

2.1   IDENTIFY THE ANGLE

The idea for your case study could come about because of specific objectives, chance encounters or the development of random thoughts. Often, case writers discover case ideas because of:

- Something interesting that they have read which they want to examine further
- An organisation or person that they know with a story that is worth telling
- The need to develop course materials for training
- A research project that they are working on
- The threat of a gradual loss of tacit knowledge and institutional memory within an organisation

2.1.1   Identify the Central Idea

Simultaneously, as you determine the purpose of the case study, ask yourself why this would be an interesting or useful topic to write about. The perspective or view point which you choose to focus the story is known as the angle of the story. It is the premise and slant that you base your content on so that it is unique and fresh. Some call it the hook because this is what draws in your readers. Others call it the big idea because it is the main controlling idea of your case study.

To determine the angle of the case study, you will have to conduct some initial research. For a start, read up whatever you can find about the topic, organisation or key persons related to the topic. Search the Internet for information, read up industry- or trade-specific publications, media reports or books written about the organisation or person you want to write about. As you read, constantly ask yourself why this would make an interesting topic to write about. If there is already a lot of information in the public space, ask yourself how what you intend to write will add value to the existing pool of information.

During research for the case study "Growing a City in a Garden"[1], the authors identified two possible story angles using the same bundle of information. One angle was to tell the story of greening Singapore (Fig. 2.2a) while the other angle was the story of urban governance (Fig. 2.2b).

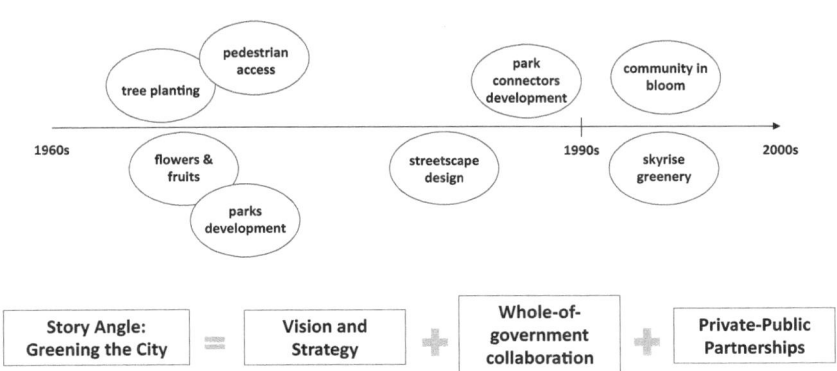

Fig. 2.2a   Story angle: *Greening the City*

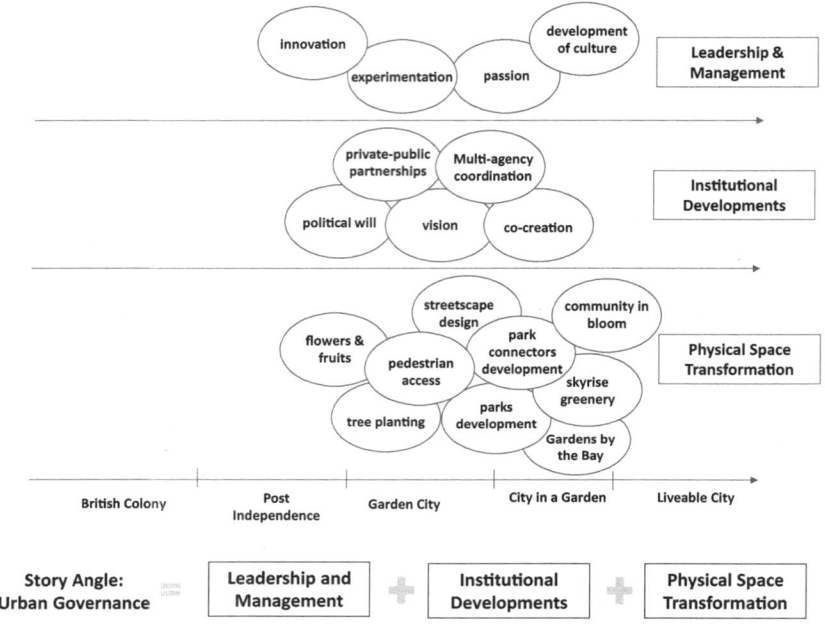

Fig. 2.2b   Story angle: *Urban Governance*

The angle on greening Singapore told the story of Singapore's transformation into a garden city. It explained the rationale of strategies behind developing greenery in the city and described how these strategies were implemented over a 50-year period. The second angle on urban governance narrated the story of Singapore's urban governance strategies by highlighting parallel developments of physical space, institutions and the actions of leaders. The second angle was developed while researching on the first angle of the case study. The authors found the second angle interesting for readers who were interested in urban development and planning.

2.1.2   Compelling Idea

The case study angle is important because it defines what and how you write your case study, and therefore, how you would structure your content. The case study angle becomes compelling when there is an element of surprise or unexpected development. These can be brought out by the tensions, complications and challenges of the event or issue that you are describing.

Take time to research it, understand it and think about the angle and purpose of your case study. If flawed, the other parts will crumble. When looking for an angle and purpose for your case study, here are some questions that you should ask yourself:

- How is this case study different from what is already known or available publicly? Will you be able to write this case study in an original way that makes it different from other similar case studies?
- What is the central conflict in the story that you are planning to write?
- Is the cause and effect pathway simple or complex?
- Will readers care about, identify with or benefit from the story in the case study?
- How do things change at the end of the case study? Is there a solution to the problem?
- Will the case study create some sort of change in the reader (e.g. change their behaviour, introduce new perspectives, generate new knowledge, challenge their assumptions or stimulate a call to action)?
- Will readers enjoy reading this case study and find it meaningful?
- If you are writing this case study for teaching purposes, does it meet your curriculum needs, teaching objectives and learning outcomes?
- Is it possible to write this case study? What has to happen in order to make this possible?

Identifying an angle for your case study can be time consuming. Do not be discouraged. Often, a good test of whether you are clear about the angle and purpose of your case study is to answer these two questions:

- *What is the main idea of your case study?*
- *Can you describe your entire case study in a single sentence?*

To look for an interesting angle and determine the purpose for your case study, talk to experts, critics and industry watchers. Ask for their views and observations to determine if there is indeed an angle that would form an interesting story for learning and insights. While you make sense of your topic, look for opportunities to speak to key stakeholders from the organisation that you will be writing about to get an indication of whether they would be interested to participate in this case study project.

After conducting the initial research, you may find that there is nothing additional that is worth writing about and a new case study may not provide additional value to achieve the purpose you had in mind. It may be that the materials that you have discovered in the public domain as you were conducting your initial research could be used in its original form for your purpose. Or it may be that during your conversations with the stakeholders and organisations, you discover that they are not supportive of the case study, and that you may have to disguise the case or write from secondary sources. If so, you should ask yourself if such a case study would still be of value to readers or to the purpose of what you had in mind.

At this point, you will have to make a judgement call. You may choose to continue with the project or you may choose to abandon it. Case study projects are always resource-intensive because they require substantial time and manpower to develop. However, if you are convinced that there is value in writing a case study on the topic, then proceed to the next step which is to develop a case study concept plan.

2.2   Develop Case Concept Plan

One of the common errors of case writers is to plunge into the writing of the case study without first developing a concept plan for what they intend to write and how they intend to approach what they want to write.

Setting the scope of where you want to start and stop your story in the case study helps to focus the story to achieve your purpose. It gives clarity to the writer. More importantly, the case study concept plan is an important communication tool and terms of reference document for you to describe the purpose and angle of your case study to your stakeholders. In other words, your case study concept plan serves as an anchor for you to justify the value of your case study project and build confidence in your stakeholders about the professional manner which you will be carrying out the project.

The Case Roundel (see Chap. 3) helps case writers think deeper about how they will approach the topic and outline the scope and concept of your case study. The case concept plan is also developed in conjunction with stakeholders and used to engage them to participate in the case study project.

A writer who skips developing a comprehensive case study concept plan before writing the case study may face some of these challenges:

- Produce a case study that describes the blow-by-blow account of a situation but lacks a clear story angle. Without a clear angle, the meaning, value and insights intended that could have been captured in the case study would be lost.
- Produce a case study that is not suitable for the target audience or platform because the planning of the case study was not carefully considered.
- Face resistance from stakeholders in obtaining information and support for the case study because they could not see the value of the project. When getting approval and release for the case study, stakeholders may question what has been written and question the quality of the work, if they feel that they have not been sufficiently consulted during the project.
- Produce a case study that does not meet the original intent and purpose of the project because the writer veered off the research goals as more interesting and exciting information is revealed during the research process.

Identify Idea and Angle and *Develop Case Concept Plan* of the Writer's Compass could take up 50% of the time spent on the whole case study project. They are critical steps in the process because they anchor the case study and set the tone for the rest of the process.

2.3   RESEARCH AND ANALYSIS

Once you have received support for the case concept plan, you are now ready to build on the initial research that you did when deciding on the topic. The next step is to conduct research and make sense of the data that you collect. Because we have defined the case study as an account of a real event, person and organisation, its content must be anchored on facts and evidence, which makes research critical to the writing of the case study.

2.3.1   *Secondary Source Case Studies*

Case studies can be written from secondary data or primary data, or both. Cases that are written with only secondary data are sometimes referred to as secondary source cases. In such cases, published information is the main source of information. As case writer, you must ensure that the published source that you gather is authentic, credible and reliable since these are your only source of information. It is good practice to inform readers that this is a secondary source case by putting a qualifier in the footer of the front page of the case study stating that 'This case study was written based on published information.'

A common misconception is that secondary source cases are easier to write compared to primary source cases. This is not true because finding accurate, reliable, valid and credible information to support the story that you are telling can be more difficult than hearing the facts directly from the respondent that you are interviewing. The case writer of a secondary source case must be as resourceful as the case writer for a primary source case.

2.3.2   *Primary Source Case Studies*

Case studies that are written using both secondary and primary data are also referred to as field case studies because field research is conducted in the process of writing the case study. Quantitative (surveys, questionnaires, etc.) and qualitative research methodologies (primarily interviews and observation) are used in developing field cases. These cases take longer to write due to the amount of time involved in conducting field research, particularly in conducting interviews, which are fundamental to case study research.

Looking for authentic and relevant information is challenging. Besides just writing the case study, you need skilled interview techniques and an aptitude to engage stakeholders to share behind-the-scenes, in-depth and tacit information with you. These cannot be gathered through questionnaires and surveys. Field-based cases are richer and have the potential of developing new insights because of these first-hand information from respondents.

2.4   Write

The purpose of writing is to take the reader to a new level of cognition and empathy. Cognitive psychologist Ronald T. Kellogg declared that it could take at least two decades for a writer to achieve professional levels of writing skill.[2] He demarcated writing development into three macro-stages: knowledge-telling in the first 10 years, knowledge-transforming in the next 10 years and knowledge-crafting after 20 years.

In the knowledge-telling stage, the writer generates text to say what he/she intends to say. The text is often a restatement of the writer's thoughts. In the knowledge-transforming stage, the writer produces text that constitutes knowledge stored in long-term memory. The text produced is a condensed version of the writer's thought processes. In the knowledge-crafting stage, the writer progresses to professional level of expertise. The writer shapes what to say and how to say it with full consideration of how the reader will interpret the written text.

Kellogg (2006) explained, 'To effectively interpret the text from the reader's point of view, the author is forced to think about and decide what knowledge the reader already knows that need not be made explicit in the text.'[3] As the writer becomes more experienced in writing and as the writer's skill deepens, the relationship between writer, text and reader becomes stronger.

To improve and develop expert levels of writing skill requires deliberate practice. Case writers need to be intrinsically motivated to write, constantly seek feedback for their writing and keep writing. It takes a lot of hard work, skill, knowledge, experience and effort to make a case study appear effortlessly put together. But when you achieve this, you would make a difference to how readers perceived, understood and felt about themselves and their world.

Many have mistakenly associated complexity of a case study with its length. A skilful writer can unfold the most complex story with the least number of words and in the most reader-friendly manner. A case study that is complex and insightful while containing sufficient context, can be told within six to eight pages.

Depending on how the case study is to be used and circulated, the completed case study is formatted to fit the platform in which it will be used. If used for publication in a book, magazine or journal, the case study should follow the style guide of the publication and be formatted for that purpose. If used as a multimedia or video case study, the document should be re-written into a script with a storyboard. Often, a case study may be adapted or customised for different purposes. The Chronicler's Rune in Chap. 6 explains in greater detail the craft of writing.

2.5   Review and Refine

Once a draft of the case study has been written, send it to the key stake-holders of the case study project that you had identified earlier. You may want to invite subject matter experts to comment on your case study. Subject matter experts can be practitioners of a specific field related to the subject covered in the case study, or simply stakeholders who are representatives of the organisation you are writing about.

2.5.1   Requesting for Feedback

Always offer a first draft of the case study to the representative of an organisation only after face-to-face meetings and interviews with key personnel of the organisation (if it is a primary source case). Writers should avoid giving organisational representatives a partial draft of the case study within the first few weeks of contacting the organisation, especially if correspondences had been conducted largely through emails. Organisations respond better if their representatives understand the case writer's interest, sense their sincerity and recognise their efforts in finding out about their organisation's operations and culture before showing them a draft of the case study. Spending time with the organisation and its representatives helps build trust and respect between the case writer and the organisation which becomes critical when the case writer invites the organisation for feedback and to obtain the eventual release of the case study.

Where possible, develop a broad case editing rubric to guide editors and reviewers. Ask them to comment on the content as well as the structure based on the case study concept that you have developed. These should include these key elements:

- Objectives stated in the case study concept are met.
- Context of the situation frames the case study.
- Issues presented are clear.
- Information included are relevant and valid.
- Alternatives, consequences and rationales have been sufficiently discussed.
- Language and presentation are reader-friendly.

The feedback from reviewers such as stakeholders from participating organisations and subject matter experts tend to focus more on the accuracy of content and less on the technicalities of language while the case editor focuses more on the latter.

2.5.2   *Piloting the Case Study*

If you are writing a teaching case, it should be facilitated in class. As writer of the case study, sit in to observe the session and gather feedback from the instructor and participant to determine if the teaching case achieved the learning outcomes. After piloting the teaching case, incorporate new information or feedback surfaced during the case study discussions into the teaching case and teaching note. See Chap. 9 on The Case Method and Chap. 10 on The Teaching Note for more details.

2.5.3   *Prototype Testing*

Do the same for a multimedia or an online case study. A prototype of the case study is uploaded on the electronic platform and readers/learners are invited to use and interact with the case study on this platform. Any bugs in the system, navigational errors or missing information can be identified at the testing stage.

In both instances, if you find that certain information in the teaching case had confused learners, or if learners needed additional information to analyse the case study meaningfully, you can take these findings to make changes and improvements to the case study.

The purpose of the review and pilot is to provide the case writer with content guidance and broad comments and to suggest content directions to improve the quality of the case study. After receiving comments from stakeholders and subject matter experts, you should consider their feedback, decide which suggestions to accept or reject, then proceed to refine the case study draft. When done, send the draft for professional editing to scrutinise the case study for its content, structure, language and style. Chapter 8 on The Editor's Rubric provides tips on how to edit a case study.

2.6   Publish and Launch the Case Study

Finally, the case study goes live. Over time, as readers, learners, instructors, stakeholders and new users read the case study, the case writer may receive additional feedback, insights or new ideas to generate new or related case studies. When this happens, you return to the first pole of the Writer's Compass and start the process again.

NOTES

1. Neo B. S., Gwee, J. and Mak, Candy. "Growing a City in a Garden" in *Case Studies in Public Governance*, Gwee, J. (ed.), Oxon: Routledge, 2012.
2. Kellogg, R.T. (2008). Training writing skills: A cognitive developmental perspective. *Journal of Writing Research*, 1(1). http://dx.doi.org/10.17239/jowr-2008.01.01.1.
3. Ibid., p. 9.

CHAPTER 3

The Case Roundel

For every goal, there is a plan.

The Case Roundel describes the key segments of a case concept plan which helps you to sharpen and organise your thinking about the case study. This is the first expression of quality for any case study project because it outlines the deliverables and expectations of writers and their stakeholders. It contains a description of what you intend to write about and how you will be approaching the project. By putting all your ideas and parameters of the case study on paper, you can better communicate your case study project to stakeholders.

The case title is at the centre of the Roundel because this is your target and goal (see Fig. 3.1). Moving outwards, the second ring describes the objectives of your case study, the scope of what you intend to cover, and a synopsis of your case story. The third ring has two parts: your target reader and stakeholders. These are people who will read your case study but have different objectives for reading it.

The third ring describes how the case study is used, its format and the estimated length or duration (if it is a multimedia or online case study) based on the profile of the reader and the nature of usage. If you are writing a teaching case, then you should also describe the subject area and conceptual models or frameworks which you will use to anchor your case discussion.

© The Author(s) 2018
J. Gwee, *The Case Writer's Toolkit*,
https://doi.org/10.1007/978-981-10-7173-7_3

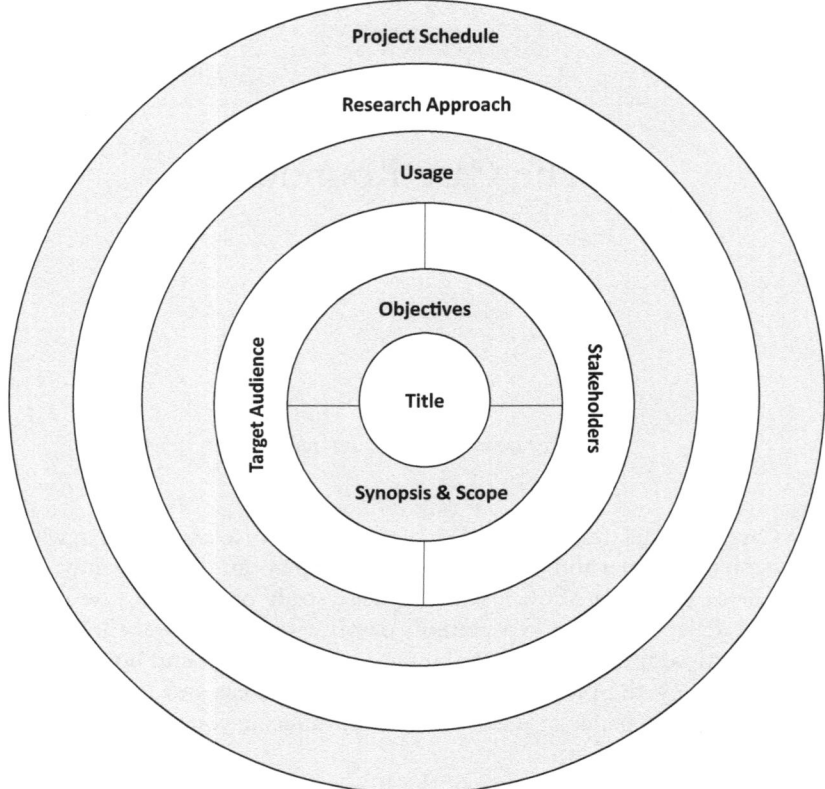

Fig. 3.1 The Case Roundel

The fifth ring describes the research approach, that is, how you intend to collect information and gather data to write your case study. Finally, the sixth and final ring of the Roundel conveys the project schedule. Each element of the Case Roundel is independent but, when combined, anchors the case concept.

3.1   [Ring 1] The Case Study Title

This is the working title of the case study. At this stage, you may or may not have a definitive title. But you should force yourself to name your case study so that it can serve as a label for your document. You can refine the title mid-way through writing, when the story is better formed, or at the end of the project where the lessons learnt give you a better idea of how you want to title the case study. Naming your case study at the start of the project is important because it defines what you want to do and focusses the rest of the elements of the case concept plan.

3.2   [Ring 2] Objectives, Synopsis and Scope

3.2.1   Case Objectives

The objectives of the case study are statements that outline the purpose of the case study. Listing a maximum of three objectives helps to focus the case study. It also helps to ensure that the case study is sufficiently rich with insights that would be interesting for the target audience. Case objectives statements are always written with a 'to' infinitive plus a verb. A verb is used to describe what happens to the reader after reading the case study. Hence, objectives are action-oriented and describe the expected outcome of the case study.

If the case study is a teaching case, then the case objectives should support and be aligned to the programme's learning outcomes since the teaching case is a pedagogical tool. In an educational context, learning outcomes express the behaviour, standard, criteria and condition of what the learner has to demonstrate as a result of analysing and discussing the teaching case. For this purpose, learning outcomes are performance statements of what the learner is expected to do, know or value after reading and discussing the case study. Specific to learning, educators are concerned with developing the learner rather than whether the case study is an excellent research or literary product.

For Pedagogy
Every educational programme is defined by a set of curriculum parameters which outline the performance criteria of learners. These serve as a yardstick to guide the instructor or facilitator how to use the teaching case. If you are writing a teaching case, you can write case objectives using verbs that are pegged to different levels of performance that you would like the learner to demonstrate. One of the commonly used performance level classification systems is Bloom's taxonomy.

Bloom's taxonomy is a classification system that was first published in 1956 to define and distinguish different levels of human cognition.[1] Named after cognitive psychologist Benjamin Bloom (1913–1999), the taxonomy was organised into three domains: cognitive, affective and psychomotor. Each domain comprised five to six classifications tiered into levels of skills and behaviour with corresponding verbs which educators use as a reference when crafting learning outcomes.

The cognitive domain is divided into six levels: level 1 is labelled 'remembering', level 2 'understanding', level 3 'applying', level 4 'analysing', level 5 'evaluating' and level 6 'creating'. The affective domain has five levels: level 1 for 'receive', level 2 for 'respond', level 3 for 'value', level 4 for 'organise' and level 5 for 'internalise'. The psychomotor domain has five levels: level 1 for 'imitation', level 2 for 'manipulation', level 3 for 'precision', level 4 for 'articulation' and level 5 for 'naturalisation'. Bloom's taxonomy is a good tool to help with choosing the right verbs to describe the level and behaviour that are expected of learners.

However, if you are writing a research or knowledge-capture case study which is not intended solely as a pedagogical tool, then the verbs that you use for your case study objectives are not constrained by the levels of performance that you want your reader to demonstrate as a learner. Here is a list of common used verbs that you can consider when writing your case objectives.

act	compose	define	explain	integrate	observe	reconstruct	state
adapt	concentrate	demonstrate	extend	interpret	outline	reference	solve
analyse	conduct	describe	extrapolate	invent	perform	refute	summarise
apply	copy	design	feel	investigate	persuade	reiterate	synthesise
assess	construct	develop	focus	invite	plan	relate	tell
appraise	contrast	devise	follow	justify	plot	replicate	test
argue	convince	differentiate	formulate	label	predict	respond	trace
articulate	coordinate	discover	generate	list	present	report	transform
ask	create	discuss	highlight	manage	propose	reproduce	translate
build	critique	distinguish	identify	manipulate	provide	rewrite	understand
challenge	curate	estimate	illustrate	master	qualify	revise	use
classify	customise	evaluate	implement	match	quantify	share	verify
combine	debate	examine	infer	measure	question	show	
compare	deconstruct	execute	influence	memorise	recall	seek	
complete	defend	experiment	initiate	modify	recognise	select	

3.2.2   *Synopsis and Scope*

A case synopsis is a summary (between 250 to 300 words) of the case study. The synopsis contains a brief highlight of the key issues or problems that will be described in the case study. As part of the description, the synopsis also identifies the main character, key players, as well as the time frame in which the narrative will be set (e.g. January 2015 to September 2016). This timeframe refers to the first trigger of action in the story and last moment that you intend to end the story. It helps the writer to organise the series of events and activities between these start and end points (also known as the cuts of the case study).

The case synopsis is the readers' first encounter with the case narrative. It should convince readers why this case study is worth reading. The case synopsis also describes the angle of the case study. The ability to write a synopsis succinctly is a test of whether you are clear about your case idea and angle. When you are precise about these two aspects of your case study, then you will be able to give an accurate and concise description. For example, if your case study is about obtaining market entry into the robotics industry, then your synopsis must capture this angle and not describe the development of the robotics cluster.

3.3   [RING 3] TARGET AUDIENCE, STAKEHOLDERS

3.3.1   *Target Audience*

Now that you have stated why you are writing the case study and provided a synopsis of its contents, the next step is to clarify who you are writing for. The target audience of your case study can refer to target readers or target learners. Your case study fulfils a specific purpose, whether it is for learning, teaching, research or knowledge-capture. Unlike fiction writing, case writers are not writing for themselves.

Hence, the objectives of a case study are inexplicably linked to the reader, and it is critical that writers have a good idea of who will be reading their case study—What are your readers' assumed knowledge, skills and behaviour? How can the case study be engaging, comprehensible and inspiring to them?

Consider the profile of your target audience to reduce any communication or information barriers that may prevent your case study from eliciting the desired response that you want from your readers. Think about their:

- current state of knowledge and intellectual framework
- beliefs, values and cultural background
- attitudes and self-concept
- level of motivation
- openness to new information and experiences
- age and life cycle stage
- highest education level
- work experience
- career stage
- language proficiency
- learning style and preferences

Research on learning styles had revealed that people acquire knowledge and absorb information in different ways. Neil Fleming's VARK model categorised learners into these four modalities of learning:[2]

- *Visual*: learn best by seeing graphic displays such as charts, diagrams, illustrations, handouts, videos and so on.
- *Auditory*: learn best by hearing information such as listening to lectures.
- *Read/write*: learn best using text-based information such as reading books, taking notes, creating PowerPoint presentations, making lists and so on.
- *Kinesthetic*: learn best by touching or doing such as manipulating objects and materials.

VARK is just one of the many theories on learning styles. In the Theory of Multiple Intelligences, Howard Gardner (1983/2003) proposed that individuals have more than one type of intelligence—'an intelligence is the ability to solve problems, or to create products, that are valued within one or more cultural settings'[3]—that is commonly measured by IQ tests. Instead individuals exhibit different types of intelligences such as musical intelligence, bodily-kinesthetic intelligence, interpersonal intelligence, intrapersonal intelligence, naturalist intelligence, existential intelligence, the intelligence of 'big questions', and pedagogical intelligence.[4]

Once you understand the learning style and dominant intelligence of your readers, you can customise your case study to better engage and communicate with them. For the same reason, you should consider how you can format and package your case study in ways that it can reach your readers. Identify different methods and platforms to do this. Depending on the amount of time and resources available, you could incorporate any of these elements to grab their attention and improve reader retention of your case study:

- colourful charts and graphs
- maps and outlines
- videos
- audio recordings
- space set aside for annotation, note-taking and reflection

The profile of target audience may affect how you present the case study. If the target audience are system engineers who are used to processing technical information, the case study may need to be presented in a more methodical manner to cater to the target audience profile and aid their learning styles.

The purpose of listing down the target audience in the case study concept plan according to the readers' job roles, level of seniority at work, education levels, and learning styles is to provide a reference point to both writers and stakeholders on how the case study should be customised to readers' profile. Ultimately, your goal as a case writer is to achieve the case study objectives and add insights or shift the mindset of your readers because of what they have read in your case study.

3.3.2   Stakeholders

Stakeholders are individuals who can affect the writing of your case study or have an interest in what you write because the contents may affect them personally or professionally. The development of the case study concept plan marks the start of stakeholder engagement, which is a critical but often overlooked aspect in the case development process. Find out who are the key decision-makers and information gate-keepers in the organisation so that you can navigate the politics and culture of your stakeholders' operating environment. They may include any or all of the following:

- the protagonist
- organisations (these could be private sector organisations, public sector organisations and non-profit organisations)
- key appointment holders in organisations (e.g. CEOs, MDs, Chairperson)
- customers
- suppliers
- employees
- programme managers
- committees
- political leaders

a. Identify stakeholders

You can start by identifying the stakeholders who will likely be involved in your project by building a table aligned to the Writer's Compass to track who and at which phase of your case study project the stakeholders would need to be involved. Assign the level of importance of each stakeholder so that you can devote appropriate efforts in cultivating them (Table 3.1).

When you contact a stakeholder, be sensitive and alert to the management and political culture of their organisation. In many organisations, there are unseen power bases and unspoken rules. Many times, case study projects are stalled, rejected or not granted release for use because of a breakdown in the engagement of stakeholders or a lack of sensitivity to the political culture of their organisations.

Table 3.1   Identify stakeholders

The Writer's Compass	Name of person involved	Nature of involvement	Level of importance (high, moderate, low)
Identify idea and angle			
Develop case concept plan	C M Lee, CEO	Case protagonist	High
Research and analysis	Jeremy Rutgers, site engineer	Technical expert	Moderate
Write			
Review and refine	C M Lee, Jeremy Rutgers	Fact check and review	High
Publish and launch			

There may be instances where you would need help from higher authorities to connect with key stakeholders. Clearly, if the person that you have identified in your case study as protagonist is not responsive to your invitation to participate in the case study, you may need to find another protagonist, re-angle your case study, and consider if the case study can be written without a protagonist. In situations where you are asked to disguise names of individuals or the organisation, you should consider if the case can work and be of value if some of the facts are disguised.

b. Engaging Stakeholders

To a certain extent, stakeholder engagement is an exercise in strategic public relations. Your goal as a writer is to convince, secure and sustain the interest of the participating organisations and individuals to support what you write. You need to cultivate an on-going relationship with both top management and middle management.

To get your stakeholders to provide the information that you need and co-own the project with you, always consider the value and benefit of the case study to them. Communicate the intent of the case study project, and obtain their feedback on the case study concept plan. Talk to them, ask them for opinions, help them to understand your intent and process, explain the benefits of the case study and what you are planning to do. At the same time, find out about their interests, the culture in which they operate, and the challenges they face.

c. Co-write or Co-develop

If there is opportunity and there are no copyright disagreements, invite them to participate in the case study project at a deeper level. For example, the organisation may like to write up a fact sheet or chronology of the organisation's history for the Annex of the case study. Or, the organisation may like to use the raw materials collected to develop a corporate exhibit for the organisation's anniversary celebrations. There is no fixed rule or formula of where the opportunity for greater stakeholder participation may be found, you will have to keep an open mind and be aware of the possibilities as you sense-make the receptiveness and motivations of your stakeholders. The greatest benefit of having your stakeholder participate in your project is that you can get much better access to information and engage in better discussions throughout the course of the case study development process.

d. Face-to-Face Kick-Off Meeting

A face-to-face meeting is the best way to gather feedback, set context and kick-off the project. During this meeting, it is important to have the writer and key decision-makers in the participating organisation meet to clarify the case development plan, discuss expectations for the project and agree on key project milestones. Issues related to copyright, ownership of intellectual property and eventual sign-off of the final draft should also be discussed. Case writers, project sponsors and stakeholders must agree on the case study concept plan because this will serve as the point of reference for the project.

The kick-off meeting is only the start of the engagement process. Throughout the entire duration of the project, the case writer should regularly engage stakeholders, particularly during the key project milestones, to sustain their interest and commitment to the case study.

3.4   [Ring 4] Usage

As you consider the target audience of your case study, concurrently identify how and where the case study will be used because this sets the boundaries of how the case study should be structured, how much content to be included and how it should be composed. Articulating how the final product will be delivered gives writers and their stakeholders a better idea of what the case study should look like.

3.4.1   Format

Case studies that are to be published in a book as part of a collection of case studies follow the editorial direction and style of the publication. Similarly, case studies that are submitted for publication in a journal comply with the requirements of the journal. Teaching cases that are used in classrooms are crafted with an engaging opening section followed by background, body and a closing that has a call to action. Video cases use a combination of text, audio and visual to deliver the story. As you consider different formats, estimate the number of pages (if for a print publication) or the duration (if for a video) that your case study should have in order for it to present the information most effectively to the target audience. The format of the case study could differ depending on how it is used.

3.4.2 Theories, Concepts and Frameworks

If your case study is used for teaching, you may want to use the teaching case to illustrate specific theories, concepts or frameworks; these should be highlighted in the concept plan to ensure that these elements are included in the final output. Similarly, case studies that are written to illustrate best practices or failures may also be anchored on specific theories and frameworks.

As you conceptualise your case study, think about how you should structure the story so that you can bring out the theories, concepts and frameworks that will be highlighted in your case study. Case editors and stakeholders can also use these to assess the completed teaching case and determine if the original intent of using the teaching case to illustrate these frameworks have been achieved. Concurrently, identify and list down keywords for your project. The key words can be used for subject classifications or as search terms to help readers locate your case study.

3.4.3 Programme

If the case study is to be used for teaching, identify the subject area covered in the teaching case and the programme which it will be used. The same teaching case can be used in several different programmes, depending on the subject area and issues covered. With the programme in mind, you may want to write out a list of three to five questions that you want your learners to think about when they read your teaching case. These questions can be used for reflection to guide the reading and analysis of the teaching case, or they can be used to anchor class discussions. The questions should reflect the issues and learning outcomes of the teaching case. They also help to focus the case content and detail to stakeholders and some of the areas that will anchor class discussions. Finally, these questions are a checking mechanism for writers to align the content to the case objectives and theoretical frameworks.

3.4.4 The Pitch

Similar to the concept of sound which is the degree of highness or lowness of tone, the pitch of a case study refers to the level of difficulty that you want to set for your case study. Your decision is based on your objectives for the case study and your target audience. Leenders et al. (2001) identified three dimensions of case difficulty: analytical, conceptual and presentation.[5] Case studies could challenge readers in any of these three dimensions, or a combination of these dimensions (Table 3.2).

Table 3.2   The three dimensions of case difficulty

Dimension	Degree of difficulty (1 is low while 3 is high)	Description
Analytical	1	To assess whether decision taken was indeed appropriate and the process followed correctly, whether further alternatives or decision criteria might have been considered and what the future consequences could be.
	2	To analyse the situation, generate additional alternatives, evaluate the alternatives against specified decision criteria, make a decision, and develop an action and implementation plan.
	3	To analyse the situation, figure out whether a decision needs to be taken and what alternatives might be considered, what decision criteria should be applied and what alternative is preferable, how it may be implemented and what the outcomes are likely to be.
Conceptual	1	To apply a single, simple theory or concept assigned in readings to a specific case problem or issue without requiring extra explanation of the theory or concept in class.
	2	To apply the appropriate theory or concepts or a single complex concept with some assistance or further discussion and explanation in class.
	3	To apply a variety of theories and concepts which may be relevant to the case issues. May require a substantial amount of assistance and explanation in class to understand the integration of theories or to explain complex theories as part of the total set.
Presentation	1	To analyse correctly a short, well-organised case containing no extraneous information, little missing information and presented in a single format.
	2	To analyse correctly a medium length case with some disorganisation, containing a medium amount of extraneous information, with some missing information and presented in a single or double format.
	3	To analyse within a reasonable length of time a long case which may be disorganised, containing lots of extraneous information, substantial amount of missing information and presented in a variety of formats (e.g. text, video).

Source: Summarised from Leenders, M.R., Maufette-Leenders, L. A. and Erskine, J. A. (1973, 1978, 1989, 2001). *Writing Cases*. London: Richard Ivey School of Business, The University of Western Ontario, pp. 18–22, 34–35.

3.5   [Ring 5] Research Approach

This item explains how the writer will research and gather information for the topic. It states whether the case study will be written based on secondary data (i.e. published sources) or primary data (i.e. data collected through field work).

For primary source case studies, writers explain in this section how they intend to collect the data and whether stakeholder participation is needed. This helps to manage the expectations of stakeholders and help them clarify their role and the extent of their involvement in the case writing project. Stakeholder concerns can then be highlighted during the start of the project which then help writers manage stakeholder expectations before the project progresses.

If, for any reason, stakeholders choose not to provide information for the case study or ask not to participate in the project after reading the case study concept plan, case writers can make a decision whether to turn the case study into a secondary source case or to abort the project. Therefore, this is an important item in the case study concept plan which case writers should take time to compose and highlight to stakeholders.

3.6   [Ring 6] Project Schedule

The project schedule outlines the milestones of key activities and the corresponding timeframes within which the activities will take place. It is a guide for writers and stakeholders to agree on specific deadlines to help the project progress smoothly. Encircling all the other elements of the Case Roundel, this final and fifth ring guides how much time can be spent on the first four rings of your concept plan. It also ensures that you hit your target.

3.7   Sample Case Concept Plan

Table 3.3 shows the case concept plan of the case study *Charting a New Course* You can read the full case study in Chap. 7 and the teaching guide in Chap. 10 customise the plan according to purpose and context. If you are developing a research case for a university project, you should follow the university's format and requirements for research proposals.

Table 3.4 helps you to think about your case study as you apply the Case Roundel.

Table 3.3   Case study concept plan

Title of case study	Charting a New Course
Synopsis and scope	As the trend of privatisation moved into the Asia Pacific in the mid-1990s, many industries had to re-invent themselves. One of the changes was the deregulation of the telecommunications industry. This case study describes the challenges confronted by telephone directory publisher, SingTel Yellow Pages. It will highlight the opportunities and threats faced by SingTel Yellow Pages, as well as examine the company's strengths and weaknesses. This case study will identify the company's key considerations when re-inventing itself.
Case objectives	• To assess the telecommunications industry and identify the opportunities and threats that it presents to SingTel Yellow Pages. • To evaluate the strengths and weakness of SingTel Yellow Pages and the value that the organisation can create. • To propose new strategies and business model for SingTel Yellow Pages in a deregulated telecommunications industry.
Target audience	• Undergraduate and postgraduate students • Students in executive development programmes • Participants in corporate training programmes
Stakeholders	• SingTel Yellow Pages • SingTel Group

Usage	Publication
	  • Case study for knowledge-capture
	  • Teaching case
	Distribution
	  • For publication in journal (estimated 12 pages)
	  • Reading material for programmes (10 pages)
	  • For knowledge management portal (25 pages)
	Programmes
	  • Strategic Management 101
	  • New Employee Induction Programme
	The pitch
	  • Analytical level 2
	  • Conceptual level 1
	  • Presentation level 2
	Subject area
	  • Strategy development
	  • Business management
	  • Telecommunications industry liberalisation
	Questions for reflection
	  1. Analyse SingTel Yellow Pages's strengths and weaknesses in the face of deregulation.
	  2. Explain SingTel Yellow Pages's value chain and describe how this can help it create sustainable competitive advantage?
	  3. How can SingTel Yellow Pages differentiate? What options does it have to respond and survive in a liberalised market?

(continued)

Table 3.3   (continued)

Research method	Secondary research • literature review using annual reports, books and corporate publications Primary research • in-depth interviews with veterans, experts, partners and decision-makers
Project schedule	Secondary research: January Kick-off meeting with SingTel Yellow Pages stakeholders: April In-depth interviews: April to July Analysis and writing: August to October Review and refine: November Case Release: December Publication/Pilot in class: December

Table 3.4   Template for Case Concept Plan

Case Title

Title of case study: _____

Nature of case study (please choose one):
□ New case study   □ Update of an existing case study

Type of case study (choose all or any that apply):
□ Teaching Case   □ Research Case   □ Documentation Case for Knowledge Capture

Case Synopsis

Please provide a 250 to 300-word description of the key issues, the angle of the case study
and explain why this case study is unique. Highlight also the timeframe covered in the case
study.

(*continued*)

Table 3.4   (continued)

Case Objectives
Please list down three objectives of your case study.
1.
2.
3.

Target Audience

Occupation type:
☐ undergraduate students   ☐ post graduate students
☐ students in executive education   ☐ professionals, managers, executives
☐ specialists and technical personnel   ☐ academia
☐ others:

Age:
☐ 19 – 25 years old   ☐ 26 – 35 years old   ☐ 36 – 45 years old
☐ 46 – 59 years old   ☐ 60 years and above

Highest education level:
☐ Certificate   ☐ Diploma   ☐ Undergraduate   ☐ Postgraduate

English language proficiency (written and oral):
☐ native   ☐ fluent   ☐ basic   ☐ nil

Dominant learning style (for teaching case):
☐ visual   ☐ auditory   ☐ read & write   ☐ kinesthetic

Usage

Delivery format & length/duration:
☐ print; estimated no. of pages (with exhibits): _____
☐ multimedia; estimated duration (minutes): _____
☐ video; estimated duration (minutes): _____
☐ audio; estimated duration (minutes): _____

Delivery platform:
Public
☐ print publication   ☐ Internet   ☐ learning management system
Internal
☐ print publication   ☐ Intranet   ☐ knowledge management system
☐ restricted access

(continued)

Table 3.4   (continued)

Research Method

Secondary sources:
□ Corporate materials   □ Public sources (e.g. from libraries, online databases, Internet)

Primary sources:
□ In-depth interviews   □ Observation
□ others, pls specify: _____

Please describe how the above will be obtained:

Project Schedule	Apr	May	Jun	Jul	Aug	Sep	Aug
Develop case concept							
Research							
Analysis							
Write							
Publish							

If you are writing a teaching case, the case concept plan should include these items:

Subject Area and Name of Programme

Subject area(s) covered in the case study: _____
_____

Name of course(s) that case study will be used: _____
_____

Conceptual Frameworks and Theories

Please briefly highlight the concepts and theories that will be covered in the case study.

(*continued*)

Table 3.4   (continued)

Questions for Reflection and Discussion
Please list down the questions you want readers to think about.
1.
2.
3.
4.
5.

Learning Design
Teaching approach: □ large group discussion   □ small group discussions followed by group presentations □ combination of the above □ others, please specify:

A good case concept plan fulfils these criteria:

- the objectives of the case study are clearly identified and articulated
- the angle explored in the case is interesting and has learning value
- the issues described are current, relevant and/or evergreen
- the case study has the potential for new insights and perspectives

If used in a programme, then a good case concept plan is one where the learning outcomes are aligned with subject area, programme parameters and target learner profiles.

NOTES

1. Hidden curriculum (2014, August 26). In S. Abbott (Ed.), The glossary of education reform. Retrieved on 2017, January 19, from http://edglossary.org/blooms-taxonomy/.
2. Fleming, N.D (April 2012), *Teaching and Learning Styles: VARK Strategies*. (Christchurch: Neil D Fleming, April 2012). Accessed on July 6, 2017 from http://vark-learn.com/wp-content/uploads/2014/08/VARK-Teaching-and-Learning-Styles.pdf.
3. Gardner, H. *Frames of mind. The theory of multiple intelligences.* (New York: BasicBooks, 1983/2003), p. x.
4. Gardner, H, "Frequently asked questions – multiple intelligences and related educational topics", accessed on January 23, 2017 from https://howard-gardner01.files.wordpress.com/2012/06/faq_march2013.pdf.
5. Leenders, M.R., Maufette-Leenders, L. A. and Erskine, J. A. (1973, 1978, 1989, 2001). *Writing Cases.* London: Richard Ivey School of Business, The University of Western Ontario.

CHAPTER 4

The Research Rhombus

Within the chaos of information, we organise the random to reveal
new knowledge, keen insights and fresh ideas.

The Research Rhombus illustrates the activities of research that are necessary for analysis and the development of insights (Fig. 4.1). The strict properties that give rhombus[1] its form remind us that this part of case development requires precision and rigour. Yet, while research needs to be exacting, the slant of two of its parallel sides reminds us that research is also dynamic. This is because research is also a journey where the information is always moving. Nothing is a single event, everything is interconnected. Therefore, the research rhombus can be tugged and pulled into a square or diamond, depending on your research design and where the information leads you. The research that you carry out on a topic helps you to frame the content of your case study. By scaffolding your research process, you move closer to discovering information and gathering knowledge that will develop insights for your case study.

Secondary research is a broad-based activity. It is the outer-most shell of the Research Rhombus because you need to cast your net wide to consider all the potential and relevant sources of secondary data about your topic. This is followed by primary research because although secondary research may be extensive and intense, you are considering very targeted sources of information and drilling deeper into them with specific goals. Analysis of the data that you have collected requires deep

© The Author(s) 2018
J. Gwee, *The Case Writer's Toolkit*,
https://doi.org/10.1007/978-981-10-7173-7_4

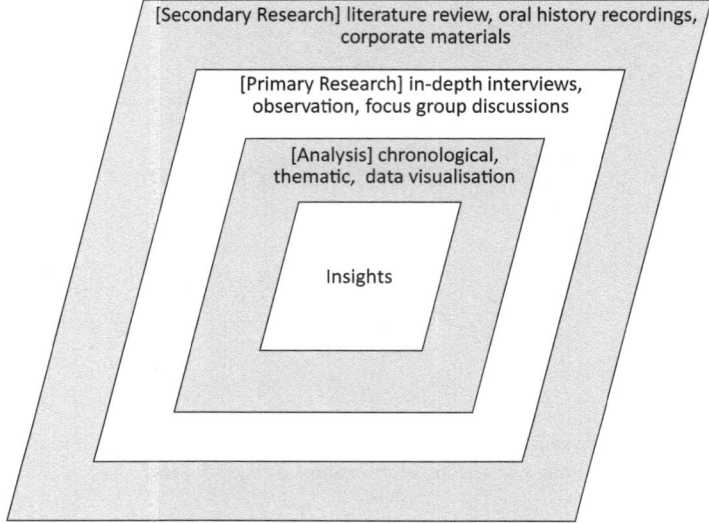

Fig. 4.1   The Research Rhombus

introspection, critical thinking and combing through the information with a great deal of detail. Therefore, analysis is closest to the core of the Research Rhombus where insights are formed. The development of insights is your goal in research because this is what you use to craft the content of your case study and achieve its objectives.

There are three types of information sources that you can collect to build your case study: primary, secondary and tertiary. Primary sources refer to raw data that is collected first-hand, such as through observation, interviews, surveys and so on. Secondary sources refer to data that is generated and written after analysis of primary data. Research reports, monographs or books that were written based on the analysis of evidence collected through primary research are all secondary information sources. Tertiary sources refer to publications that synthesise and report on secondary sources for general readers. Often, these are in the form of books, articles, textbooks, Web articles and so on.

If you are writing a primary case study or research case study, primary source information is preferred over secondary and tertiary source information because these give you first-hand information of the issues that you are studying.

Table 4.1   Information map

Type of information	Data source			Level of importance of information (high, moderate, low)	Classification of information (open, secret, confidential)
	Collection method (in-depth interview, focus group, observation, literature review, etc.)	Location of source (name of organisation, library, database, etc.)	Name of contact and designation		
Primary	In-depth interview	SingTel Yellow Pages Pte Ltd	Amelia Lindt, CEO	High	Open
Secondary	Data Analytics of Markets and Products	SingTel Yellow Pages	Amelia Lindt, CEO, SingTel Yellow Pages	Moderate	Confidential
Tertiary	Annual Report	SingTel Yellow Pages	John Tan, Public Relations Manager	Low	Open

Primary sources may be relatively less important if you are writing a secondary case study where you are dependent on good quality secondary and tertiary information. Between the two, secondary information is preferred over tertiary information because they contain direct analysis of primary data—the authors of secondary information are not reporting on another person's analysis but are drawing conclusions from the data itself.

Before you start your data collection journey, map out the type of information that you will need to collect, where the information is found, how you plan to access the information, how you will classify the information and the level of importance of that information (Table 4.1). This will help you better track the source of data as your research progresses.

4.1   Secondary Research

A common first step for many writers is to conduct a literature review of the topic that you want to write about, this means looking for secondary and tertiary sources of information. Now that you already have the case concept plan, the literature review should be done quite efficiently and in a targeted manner.

4.1.1   *Streamlining Your Research*

Search engines can turn up endless resources or none at all. Selecting the right key words and conducting advance searches can help to narrow down the search. Although search engines are the most convenient gateway of information, they may not provide the most effective results because the types of information generated are too broad.

Different from when you were first trying to pin down the angle of the case study, you are no longer engaging in exploratory research. At this stage, you should not be attempting to read the universe of materials on the topic. Instead, you should be guided by the scope of your case concept plan and be strategic in getting information that is only specific to what you intend to cover. Recognising when the information is needed, knowing where to locate it, evaluating its authenticity and relevance and using it effectively for your case study are skills that improve with practice and experience.

Depending on the topic and issue that you are writing about, you should also look for information in more specific places such as:

a. Corporate Materials

- After-action-review reports
- Annual reports
- Books (e.g. coffee table books, commemorative books)
- Concept papers
- Corporate brochures
- Corporate websites
- Financial and statistical reports
- Notes of meetings
- Newsletters
- Office Intranet
- Press releases
- Speeches

b. Materials in the Public Domain

- Blogs
- Books
- Conference papers
- Journal articles

- News articles
- Media reports
- Research reports
- Social media posts
- Subject-specific databases
- YouTube

For country-specific information, respective countries may have eResources specific to them. You can access government-specific information from sources such as:

- Official reports of parliamentary debates (e.g. Hansard)
- Oral history interviews and government records
- National newspaper archives

Gradually, add on to this initial list and build your own list of criteria to ensure that you collect only good quality information.

4.1.2   Evaluating Secondary and Tertiary Information

With each piece of secondary and tertiary information that you encounter, evaluate them against this set of basic criteria (Table 4.2).

4.2   PRIMARY RESEARCH

Compared to secondary source cases, primary source case studies are richer because they contain new perspectives that are not found in secondary materials. Primary data is most commonly gathered through in-depth interviews which remain one of the best sources of tacit knowledge. It is an effective method to mine for perspectives and knowledge of respondents who had gone through experiences first-hand. These might not have been captured in published literature and official documents. Interviews with decision-makers and resource persons[2] are a rich source of data for writing engaging case studies because they are first-hand accounts of issues and situations.

The purpose of an interview is to closely examine a specific issue, phenomenon or circumstance through the thought process and perspectives of respondents and understand why they acted or behaved the way they did. Interviews are useful because:

Table 4.2   Evaluate information sources

Evaluation criteria	Questions to ask yourself
Authenticity	Are the references (e.g. bibliography, citations) associated with the work genuine? Where else has this work been cited or quoted? Has the information been lifted or cited from another source? Who is the originator or publisher of the work? Who owns the copyright of this work?
Authority	Who is the author? Is the author a subject expert? What is the author's reputation? What is the reputation of the publisher? (e.g. university press, academic press, commercial press)
Currency	When was the information written or first uploaded? Has the information been updated? When was the information last updated?
Relevance	How many times has the work been cited or quoted by others? What are the key words indicated as part of the work? Do these relate to your purpose? What are the words listed in the index of the work?
Reliability	If taken from the Internet, what is the resource locator (.net, .gov, .org, etc.) of the work? What is the quality of references associated with the work? If taken from the Internet, are the links to other pages and websites working? Are there language errors? Are there contact details (e.g. names, emails, addresses or contact numbers) to direct queries? Is this the original source of the article or is it a report of another news source?
Objectivity	Has the work been peer reviewed? What do reviewers say of the work?

- Interviews help to identify issues that are most troubling to the person or organisation, and to understand the prevailing mental models and assumptions.
- Interviews can gather frank views, surface minority views or even contrarian and alternative views. These would not have been readily heard or observed unless rapport and trust have been established with the respondent.

- Interviews are used to validate other data, collect opinions, reflect different points of view, and gather up-to-date information.

4.2.1   Planning the Interview

One of the important roles of the case writer is to gather the tacit knowledge of respondents and translate them into explicit knowledge.

Tacit knowledge can be found in almost anyone. While researching for your case study, you may find it worthwhile talking to some of these respondents who have either deep or broad experiences, or both:

- Chairpersons
- Chief Executive Officers
- Community leaders
- Customers
- Directors
- Employees
- Heads of Departments
- Investors
- Partners
- Politicians
- Pioneers
- Project champions or sponsors
- Project experts / veterans
- Project leaders
- Supervisors
- Vendors

Deciding who to interview first depends on how much prior knowledge you have about the subject you are writing. If you are already an expert on the subject and know the industry and the organisation intimately, you would have a freer hand in deciding who to interview first. If you choose to understand the strategic vision first in order to frame the operational details that will be revealed through project managers, then interview the CEO and top management respondents first. On the other hand, if you are writing a leadership case study where you need to understand what happened on the ground before finding out why the leadership responded the way they did, you may choose to interview the CEO after speaking to the ground staff.

Remember to check the National Archives to see if there are existing oral hisotry interviews that you can tap on. This way, your interview questions can be better targeted at obtaining new information.

a. Identify the Maven

If you are at a loss on who to interview because you are unfamiliar with the industry and the topic, then you should identify the maven of the industry or organisation. The maven is a veteran or pioneer of the industry or organisation and has a wide span of experience and network. Speak to the maven, ask him to tell you about his role in the industry or organisation, the key milestones of his career which are linked to the industry or organisation and ask for his advice on who to interview. Sometimes, the maven could also link you to other respondents. Once you have spoken to the maven and have a better understanding of the subject matter, organisation and industry, you can then list down the names of other people whom you would like to speak to and decide how you would want to sequence them.

b. One-on-One Interviews

Depending on the purpose of the interview, it can be conducted with a single respondent or a group of respondents. Interviews that are conducted with a single respondent are referred to as one-on-one interviews. These are in-depth interviews that allow the respondent to share personal experiences in greater depth. One-on-one interviews are good for gathering senstive, confidential and complex data where you need details and thorough explanations to understand human actions, motivations, attitudes and value systems. For primary source case studies, it usually takes 12 to 15 interviews to gather sufficient data to identify themes and patterns.

c. Focus Group Interviews

Interviews that are conducted with a group of respondents are called focus group interviews. These usually consist of eight to ten respondents discussing a specific issue guided by the interviewer's questions. Focus group interviews are good for exploring case study ideas, new research areas or an area where it is difficult to collect data through observation. If you are uncertain about your case study idea or angle, you can use focus group interviews to obtain feedback from a group of subject matter and industry experts or practitioners, then use the information that you have collected to narrow the focus of your case study idea before conducting one-on-one interviews with specific respondents.

4.2.2 Conducting Interviews

Conducting an in-depth interview is like peeling an onion. Your first interaction with a respondent is usually fragile and tentative, just like the dry and brittle outer layer of the onion. After establishing trust with your respondent, you start to gain a deeper understanding of the issues and situation, as you urge your respondent to reveal his actions to you. Layer by layer, you unveil the external facade until you reach the core which has the sharpest and purest flavour, when respondents reveal their rationales, philosophies, feelings and innermost thoughts behind their actions.

Interviews can be categorised into structured, semi-structured or unstructured (Table 4.3). In case study research, data gathering through interviews is carried out using a semi-structured interview method. Since your goal is to gather relevant information to meet the objectives of your case proposal plan, you need to focus your questions yet allow for some flexibility during the interview for new information and tacit knowledge to emerge.

Once you have identified the respondents who will be useful for your case study, contact them to request for an interview. Use the case study concept plan that you have developed to explain the purpose of your project to them. Before the interview, research the person whom you will be interviewing so that you can focus and customise your interview questions to the profile and background of the respondent. Interview sessions should be capped at 1.5 hours to avoid respondent fatigue as well as a decline in the quality of answers given during the session.

a. An Interview Guide

Develop an interview guide to prepare yourself for the questions that you will be asking. An interview question guide generally consists of eight to ten questions. To develop the list of questions, organise your thoughts around what you would like to ask and visualise how you will be conducting the interview session. The list is called a guide because it gives you space to adapt and react to the respondent during the interview.

An interview guide sequences questions according to how you anticipate the respondent will process the questions, answer and react during

Table 4.3 Types of interviews

Type of interview	Description	Examples of interviews
Structured	In a structured interview, the interviewer controls tightly the direction of the interview. The interview questions are asked in the same manner and sequence. Consistency is critical in a structured interview because its purpose is to obtain reliable data that can be aggregated and compared. To ensure consistency in questioning techniques, interviewers: • keep to the same wording of the question in every interview session • ask questions in the same order • ask questions in the same manner • repeat the question for the respondent and avoid interpreting the question if the respondent does not understand the question. • do not add new questions or remove existing questions • accept answers only from the respondent and not another person	• one-one-one interviews • survey research interviews
Semi-structured	In a semi-structured interview, interviewers are guided by a list of questions but not constrained by the format or sequence of interview questions. Interviewers allow respondents to surface new ideas and may also tailor the questions depending on the responses received during the interview. With a less formal approach, interviewers: • prepare an interview guide which lists the broad areas and topics to be covered • ask the respondent to elaborate on the point made • ask the respondent for personal opinions • add new questions if new information surface during the interview • remove questions if deemed unnecessary • are not constrained by the order of questions	• focus group interviews • case study interviews • journalistic interviews
Unstructured	In an unstructured interview, interviewers encourage respondents to talk freely and informally about their experiences on a topic. The direction of the interview may shift as respondents speak on the topic. To encourage free flow sharing, interviewers: • allow respondents to tell their story in their own way • develop a rapport with the respondent • rarely interrupt the respondent • do not stop respondents from surfacing different and wide-ranging subjects	• narrative interviews • oral history interviews

Table 4.4   Sample interview guide

1. What are the key milestones in [name of the organisation]'s development?
2. How did the idea come about?
3. What were some of the driving forces that caused this to happen?
4. What was the significance of the strategy?
5. How was this different from previous strategies?
6. What were some of the challenges that you encountered while working on the programme?
7. What would you consider to be the critical success factors of this project?
8. If you had to do it again, what would you do differently?
9. What are some of the challenges going forward?
10. What are your priorities for the next three years?

the interview (Table 4.4). As you listen to the responses, be sensitive to body language and improvise. Sometimes, the sequence of questions may be re-ordered, or follow-up questions may have to be inserted, or some questions may need to be dropped because the respondent had already given the answer when replying to an earlier question.

According to Vogt, Brown and Isaacs, questions help to surface assumptions, clarify thinking and reframe the situation so that the researcher can have better insights to alternative perspectives.[3] A powerful question can generate curiosity, invite creativity, focus inquiry and stimulate reflective conversation. The authors identified these three dimensions to a powerful question:

- **Construction**: The phrasing, words used and linguistic architecture of a question can either open minds, narrow possibilities, stimulate thinking or cause deep reflection. For example, 'What crossed your mind when you were first asked to relocate?' asks for a different response compared to 'How were you told that you had to relocate?'
- **Scope**: Questions inform respondents the extent they should cover in their answers. It is useful to start with a narrow scope first to help focus respondents and then gradually help them broaden their answers. For example, the first question could be 'Tell me about your job', then followed by 'what does your department do?'
- **Assumption**: Inevitably, because of the specific goals of research, assumptions are embedded in the construction of questions. Case writers should guard against inserting individual beliefs and attitudes into the questions that are asked. For example, 'What should we change so that we can be world-class?' asserts the assumption that things need to change in order to be world-class while 'What can we do to be world-class?' asks for ideas and actions to be world-class.

b. Interview Techniques

An interview session can be broadly divided into three parts: the beginning, middle and end. At the start of the interview, the interviewer establishes the purpose of the interview, sets the respondent at ease and starts with general questions. The questions become more specific and thought-provoking as the interview progresses. As the session enters the end phase of the interview, focus on drawing out deeper insights from the respondent. At each phase of the interview, the types of questions asked also differ (Fig. 4.2).

These are just broad areas, always customise the tone, type and sequence of your questions to your respondents and the subject area you are writing about.

As you think about what to ask, you should be guided by these two principles:

- Will what I ask add to the content that I want to write?
- How should I ask the question to prime the accurate and authentic response?

Conducting a good in-depth interview requires skill and practice. Interviews are not simply about asking questions, it is also about listening, observing, responding and even restating information to check on the accuracy of what you are hearing. Be on your toes and focussed, always multi-tasking and trouble-shooting to ensure that the data that you are collecting is purposeful and meaningful for your case study.

To gather the best information possible, you would need good interview techniques which involve asking the right questions, summarising the questions, paraphrasing them and making use of both verbal and non-verbal reinforcers.

Ask the right questions using open-ended questions such as 'how', 'what', 'describe', 'explain' and so on. Do not influence the agenda. Allow the respondent to answer. Use situational questions to propose a scenario or idea which you would like to test out. For example, 'what would happen if...?' or 'how do you feel about...?' Probe with 'why', 'where', 'how' and 'what' questions when respondent's insights are incomplete, lacking in specifics or not sufficiently clear (Fig. 4.3). It helps to narrow the focus of discussion by requiring more detailed response.

Summarising a respondent's answer can help to repeat the key points. It also signals wrapping up one strand of thought and is a useful opportunity for the respondent to confirm your understanding or to correct any

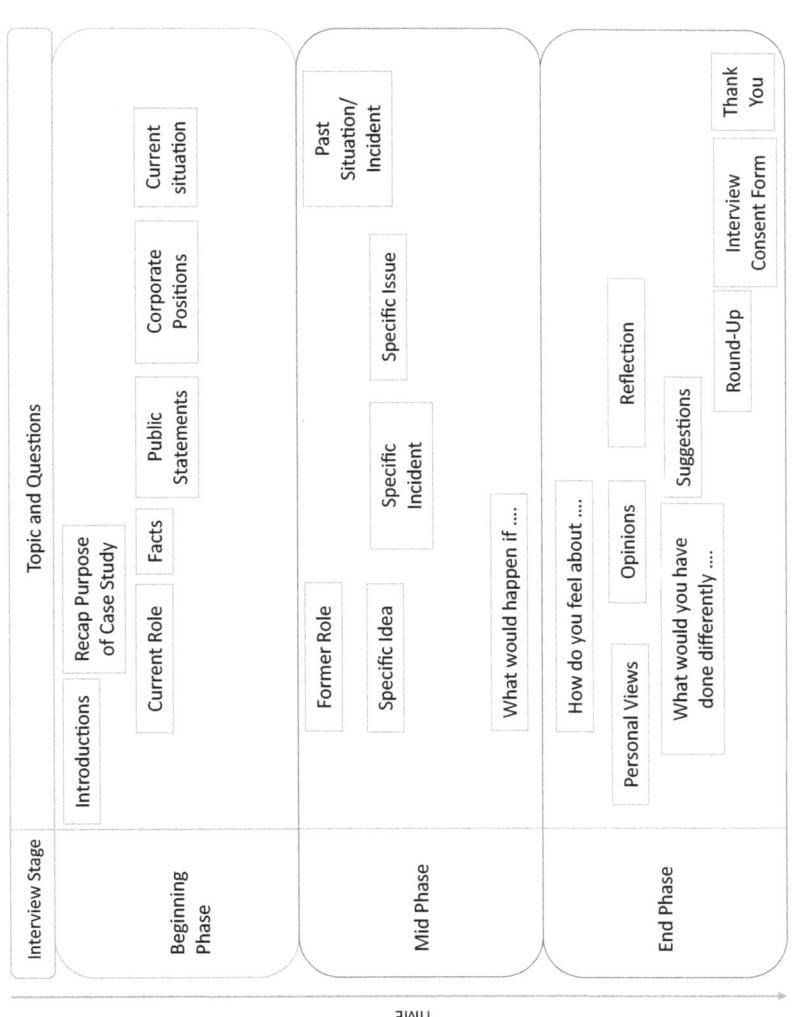

Fig. 4.2 The schematics of an interview

Interview Techniques	Dos		Don'ts
Question	Use open-ended questions: • How … • What … • Describe … • Explain … • Elaborate…	Use probing questions: • Why… • Where… • How… • Go on … • Tell me more …	• Ask binary questions – those with only Yes or No answers. • Ask many questions at one time. • Rush through the questions.
Respond	Use situational or reflective questions: • What would happen if … • If you were to do it again … • How do you feel about … • What would you do differently … • I see …		• Suggest answers to your questions. • Trivialise stories. • Judge.
Restate	Use verifying questions: • You did that because … • You mean to say … • As I understand, you meant … • Your main reasons were …		• Fear repeating your question. • Fear clarifying if you do not understand the response.
Listen and Observe	Body language: • Make eye contact • Be relax and personable	Be open-minded: • Listen for inconsistencies • Listen between the lines • Show respect	• Fear silence and pauses. • Make assumptions. • Cross arms across chest. • Fidget. • Slouch.

Fig. 4.3   Interview techniques

misunderstandings. It also restates the main thrust of a respondent's answer to open-end or probing questions.

c. Recording the Interview

One of the more effective ways of taking interview notes is to record the session. Always ask the respondent for permission to record the session before the start of the interview. Be specific about how you will be recording the session, either audio or video recording. To do that, you must first be clear about how you intend to use the information collected in the interview. The primary purpose of recording an interview is to enable transcription so that you can use it to code the data, analyse the data and look for patterns. This is an integral part of conducting qualitative research.

Interview transcripts can also be useful to extract quotes to illustrate a specific finding or add emphasis to a point that you are describing in your case study. If used for this purpose, then an audio recording can help you accurately capture what the respondent said.

If you are incorporating the interview as a component of a multimedia case study that you are putting online, then a video recording of the session may be absolutely essential to the case study.

Even if you are recording the interview, take some notes manually during the interview to pen down thoughts and observations that come to mind as you listen to the respondent. These handwritten notes may be useful during data analysis or serve as reminders to ask certain questions not previously captured in your interview guide.

Another important function of note-taking is to capture the body language that respondents may exhibit during the interview. These non-verbal cues can be worked into the interview transcript to enhance accuracy and reliability of the interview data.

4.2.3   Obtaining Respondent Consent

The respondent should sign a consent form to give you and your organisation permission to use the information provided in the interview. The interview consent form is sometimes called a release form. It authorises the case writer and/or the case writer's organisation to use the information provided by the respondent during the interview.

Use this generic consent form (Table 4.5) to customise and develop your own respondent consent forms. Always consult your lawyer when developing the consent form so that it complies with the laws and regulations of your organisation and country.

Regardless of whether the respondent signs the form, you should always inform the respondents about the benefits and risks (if any) involved in the

Table 4.5   Interview consent form

[Date]
Interview Consent Form
Permission is granted to _____ [name of case writer or the case writer's organisation] to use the information I had provided during the interview conducted by _____ [name of interviewer] on _____ [date of interview] for the research and writing of the case study specified below.

Case Study Title:	
Case Study Author/s:	
Name of Respondent:	
Address:	
Signature:	

case study, and that their participation is strictly voluntary which means that they can terminate the interview at any time, for any reason.

4.3   ANALYSIS

Research and analysis happens concurrently. With each piece of information that you access, consider its significance and simultaneously think about how you will use it in your writing. As you retrieve the information that is relevant to what you want to write, organise them into meaningful bundles with their respective sources, in anticipation that you may have to cite them in the case study. To help you keep track of the types of data that you will be collecting and their significance, you may want to create a summary table which you can use throughout the collection process. At the same time, if the data that you are collecting is classified secret or confidential, you should take note so that you can get the necessary permissions should you choose to include these in your case study (Table 4.6).

As you make sense of the information that you have collected, constantly ask yourself if there are missing or contradictory data. If you are writing a secondary source case study—one that does not contain interviews with specific respondents—you should ensure that there is breadth and depth in the sources that you cite. The mix of secondary and tertiary sources in your case study demonstrates that your case study has considered different sources of information and has rigour in its content. Although easy to understand, tertiary sources could be overly simplified

Table 4.6 Overview of data sources

Types of Data Collected (primary / secondary data)	Source of Data (name of organisation / executive / committee)	Classification of Data (open, confidential, restricted, secret)	Permission Required (Yes / No)

and may not have sufficient depth of analysis. Academic scholars and subject matter specialists may not trust your content or view what you write as credible if you only use tertiary sources in the case study.

If your case study is based solely on secondary and tertiary information sources, you should inform readers by inserting the line: 'This case study was written from public sources', in the footer of the case study.

For a start, list down all the issues, challenges and problems that are central to the case study. These will help to rein in the ideas which will eventually form part of the case study storyline. At the same time, identify the main 'actors' of the event or issue. These are people or organisations directly involved in the issue or event.

You may choose to organise the information chronologically or by themes, depending on what your research reveals to you. One of the easier ways to understand an organisation, industry, incident or protagonist is to develop a chronology of the events that occurred within the period that you are writing about. The timeline could be listed down in terms of week, month or year, depending on the period covered in your case study. The chronology forces you to list the key milestones and organise your own thinking about the subject matter. Once you have pinned down the key milestones, you can start to grow the events and things that happened under each of these key milestones by inserting the information you had collected during your research (Table 4.7).

4.3.1   Clustering data by chronology

The chart will give you a clearer view of the issue that you would like to drill down further. You can easily add in extra rows to build in sub-issues that you believe would be worth exploring. If you are writing a teaching case, this chart can help you decide on the discussion questions that you would like students to consider.

When you translate this chronology into a case study structure, it can appear like this:

Introduction
Day 1: Saturday, March 11, 2017
Day 2: Sunday, March 12, 2017
Day 3: Monday, March 13, 2017
Day 4: Tuesday, March 14, 2017
Day 5: Wednesday, March 15, 2017
Conclusion

Table 4.7 Analysis by chronology

Issue/s	Key player/s	Options	Action/Decision	Rationale	Outcome
2003, Phase 1					
Issue 1					
First case of Severe Acute Respiratory Syndrome (SARS) infection in Hong Kong	Department of Health of the Hong Kong Special Administrative Region Government	1. Legislation 2. Prevention and control 3. Public education	A combination of all the options	There were health, social, economic and humanitarian implications.	Action was insufficient to curb the spread of the disease.
Issue 2					
Issue 3					
Issue 4a					
Issue 4b					

4.3.2   Clustering data by themes

Another way to make sense of the information that you had collected is to categorise them into specific themes and align them to your case angle. Using the case study *Charting a New Course* in Chap. 7, key themes of leadership, strategy, customer experience, operations and infrastructure and service delivery were identified and mapped against the timeline of the organisation's development (Fig. 4.4).

When you translate the thematic clusters into a structure, it will appear like this:

Integrated Information Pte Ltd
The Telephone Directory Publishing Industry in Asia
Customers
Competition
Substitutes
Suppliers
Database
Strategic Options
Rethinking Strategy and Business Model
Conclusion

4.3.3   Clustering data by chronology and theme

Some stories are best told in a chronological manner while others combine a chronology within themes for a better story line. In the *Growing a City in a Garden* case study, the narrative for Part 1 of the case study was sequenced according to three broad periods of development: 1959 to early 1980s, 1980s to mid-1990s and mid-1990s onwards. A broad theme described each of these periods: the 1959 to early 1980s period was labelled Envisioning the Garden City, the 1980s to mid-1990s period was described as Beyond the Green Mantle and the mid-1990s period onwards was titled as A City in a Garden (Table 4.8). Under each of these main headers, the content was organised thematically.

If your case study is based on a specific framework, then you should think about the information that you have collected based on the components of that framework. Once you determine the categories, all you have to do is to organise how you think about and analyse your data along the categories that you have selected.

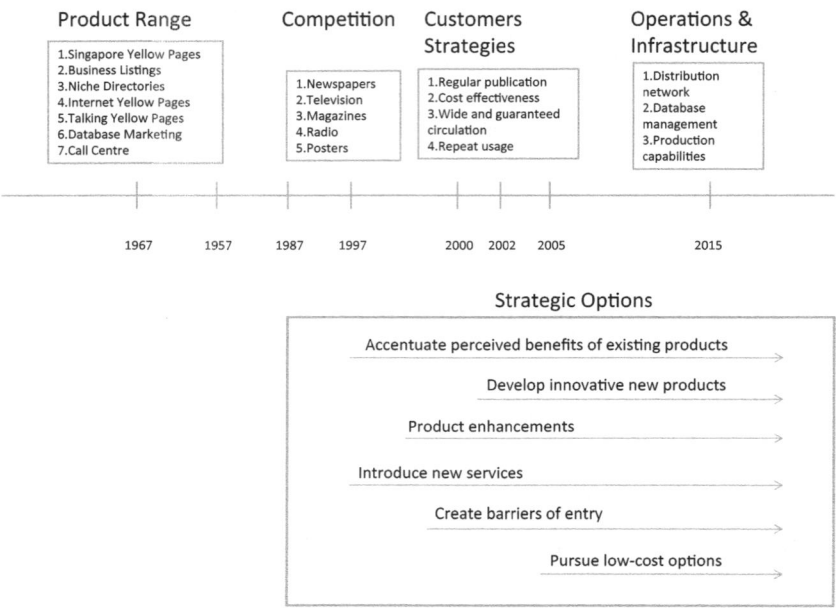

Fig. 4.4 Thematic analysis of *Charting a New Course*

Table 4.8 Combining themes and chronology within a single structure

---

PART 1: DEVELOPING GARDENS
Envisioning the Garden City (1959—early 1980s)
    Greening of Concrete Structures
    Beautifying High Visibility Places
    Planting on Reclaimed Land
    Greening of Housing Estates
    Keep Singapore Clean
    Parks for Recreations
Beyond the Green Mantle (1980s—mid 1990s)
A City in a Garden (mid 1990s onwards)
    A Park for Everyone
    Gardens by the Bay
    Streetscape Greenery Master Plan
    Park Connector Network
    Skyrise Greenery
    Waterbodies
    Community in Bloom

Source: Headings were extracted from the case study "Growing a City in a Garden" published in Neo B. S., Gwee, J. and Mak, Candy. "Growing a City in a Garden" in *Case Studies in Public Governance*, Gwee, J. (ed.), Oxon: Routledge, 2012.

4.3.4   Clustering data using data visualisation

Another method of data analysis is to visualise your data by using tools such as affinity diagrams and mind maps to organise the information and ideas. Here are some simple steps to visualise your data:

a. Write down each idea on a piece of post-it paper or a card. Keep to one idea per card.
b. After all the ideas have been written down, look for ideas that seem to be related and group them.
c. Do this until all the ideas belong to a group. Label or code the groups.
d. If the groups can be sorted further into sub-groups or to form larger clusters, arrange them accordingly.
e. Read each statement again and underline the key phrases or words.
f. Decide how you want to categorise the diagram that you have created.

Figure 4.5 shows the analysis of my case research on art and design of the Régie Autonome des Transports Parisiens.

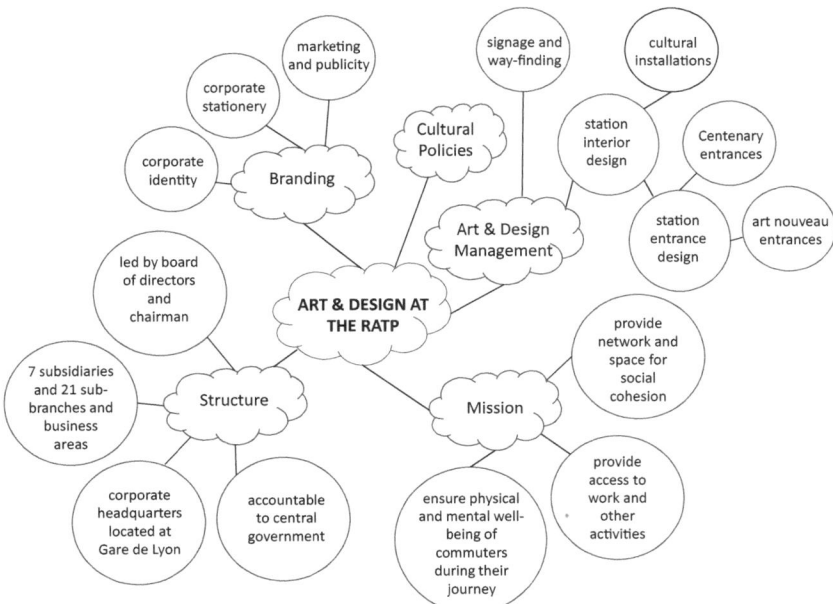

Fig. 4.5   A visual map of Art and Design of the Régie Autonome des Transports Parisiens

The goal of organising your information into milestones, themes and information clusters is to help surface patterns. The patterns that you discover produce insights that will enrich the way that you eventually present and reveal the information to readers. Similarities are clustered and differences are highlighted. After assembling the data, look for themes and extract pertinent information.

4.3.5   *Analysing Interview Data*

Similar to how you cluster data to look for patterns, do the same for the interview transcripts and notes:

- Prepare a written summary, note cards and/or outline of the key points discussed in the interview that are relevant to your topic.
- Consider the perspective provided by the respondent. How does it differ from your perspective prior to the interview?
- Note down the respondent's account about the lifestyles, culture, political atmosphere, economic issues, education and so on of the period that is being studied.
- Establish if the respondent was a dependable source of information. Did the respondent have a difficult time remembering dates, places and events?
- Compare and contrast the information given to you by the respondent with the factual information you have learned from researching other primary and secondary sources.
- List the information that is useful for the development of your case study.
- Determine how the information will contribute to the development or analysis of your case study. If there is incorrect information or biased viewpoints, how can these be used?
- Decide if the information gained from your interview can be most effectively used for your case study.

The interviews and information collected can be extracted and incorporated into the case study by inserting direct quotes, by paraphrasing what was said, or by summarising ideas.

- **Quote**: Quote the respondent if you choose to use what was said as evidence to back up statements and issues that you are writing about.

These can be words from a figure of authority or an expert. Or, it could be views that are contrary to what has been stated. Sometimes, these reveal the thinking of the respondent in his or her own words which add colour to the case study. Always ensure that you quote within the context of what was said and do not misquote.

- **Paraphrase**: If you would like to represent what had been said but express it in a better way, you may choose to paraphrase what the respondent said. When paraphrasing, do not just change one or two words. Replace most words and phrasing with your own.
- **Summarise**: Sometimes, it is better to simply highlight the gist of all that has been said. This is useful in situations where you only need related contexts or views and not the details, providing quotes for only the significant ideas.

4.3.6   Consistency and Alignment

As you categorise your findings, constantly check for alignment in these two areas: internal consistency of data and constructive alignment between your analysis with the purpose of the case study.

a. Internal Consistency

To ensure that there is internal coherence in the data, use triangulation method to cross check the data collected from two or more sources. For example, verify that your data collected from public sources is consistent with corporate data, and from the respondent's answers. This way, you can avoid biases and improve the validity and reliability of your data. It also helps to overcome over-dependence on a single method and single researcher's perspective.

b. Constructive Alignment

As you look for patterns in the data, constantly check back with your case study concept plan where you had identified the angle of the case study, its objectives, intended target audience and intended delivery style. Your analysis should meet the purpose of the case study.

These are just some basic ways to sense-make and analyse the data that you have collected. If you are using case studies as an empirical inquiry in research, your approach to data analysis will be more complex and, in some instances, require greater depth. This is because analysis should link data to research propositions and criteria in which findings are to be interpreted. Mapping meaning from data might involve various elements such as looking for meaning in events, symbols and experiences.

NOTES

1. All sides of a rhombus are congruent. Opposite angles are also congruent while consecutive angles are supplementary. The diagonals of a rhombus bisect the angles and are perpendicular bisectors of each other.
2. These are subject matter experts who may offer fresh perspectives on issues.
3. Vogt, E, Brown, Juanita, and Isaacs, D, *The Art of Powerful Question: Catalyzing Insight, Innovation and Action*, (Whole Systems Associates, Oct 2003).

PART III

Form

CHAPTER 5

The Case Jigsaw

There is a pattern to stories,
you just have to know how to put the pieces together.

Now that you have a clear case study concept, the next step is to construct your case study using the Case Jigsaw (Fig. 5.1). The Case Jigsaw helps you to build your story one piece at a time until your case study takes shape.

The Case Jigsaw is divided into three parts: Beginning, Middle and End. This is shown on the left side of the Jigsaw. The Jigsaw itself has seven independent pieces: Opening; Context; Incidents, Events, Actions; Issues and Goals; Tensions; Closing; and End Matter. The Opening and Context belong to the first part of the Jigsaw, otherwise called the Beginning. The Beginning pulls the reader into your story and sets the stage for the rest of the content. The next three pieces—Incidents, Events, Actions; Issues and Goals; and Tensions—form the Middle part of the case study. This is where the action is described in detail. It should comprise 80% of your case study. Finally, the Closing and End Matter round up the story at the End.

As you develop each of these seven pieces of your story puzzle and place them in the sequential and logical manner of Beginning, Middle and End, a structure will emerge.

© The Author(s) 2018
J. Gwee, *The Case Writer's Toolkit*,
https://doi.org/10.1007/978-981-10-7173-7_5

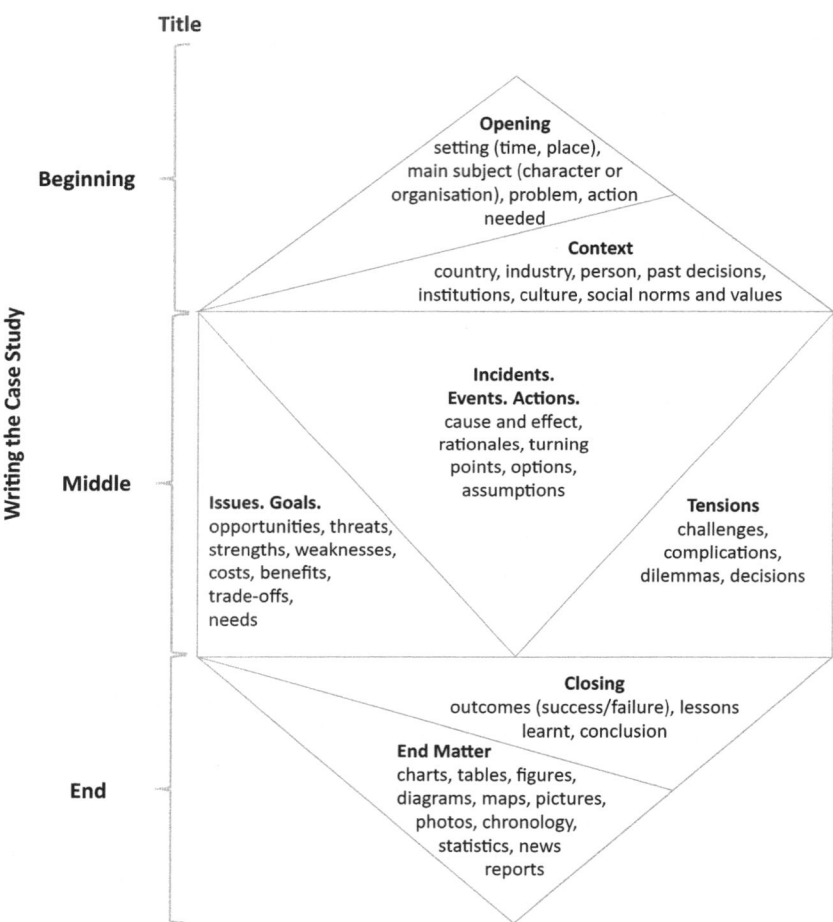

Fig. 5.1 The Case Jigsaw

5.1   THE CONCEPT OF THE CASE JIGSAW

5.1.1   The Monomyth

The structure of Beginning, Middle and End is strongly associated with the work of mythologist and writer Joseph Campbell. Campbell developed a theory of the story called the monomyth which described the journey or quest of a main character, also known as the hero of the story.[1] He explained that the standard path of a hero's journey is depicted in his rites of passage in three stages: a call to adventure, trials and victories of initiation and finally, return and reintegration with society.[2] During journey, the hero treks from equilibrium to disequilibrium and then back to equilibrium. As the hero goes through the rites of passage, he/she acquires new knowledge about himself/herself and his/her world and undergoes a personal transformation. In the same way, readers accompany the hero on his/her quest, live vicariously through his/her exploits, acquire new insights and are transformed.

5.1.2   Reading the Case Study

The concept of the Case Jigsaw came about because of reader habits and behaviour which are shown by dotted lines on the right side of Jigsaw (Fig. 5.2). When given a case study, readers tend to first establish the broad issues by reading the title, introduction, conclusion, headings and sub-headings. Their natural instinct is to look for signposts that can help them make sense of the content quickly. Hence, they read the title, headings, charts, exhibits, introduction and conclusion, while skimming the rest of the content. Visual readers will gravitate to the charts, exhibits and diagrams to look for data to help them make sense of the subject matter.

Once readers decide to read further, they will start to identify the key issues, problems and people involved in the situation. Actively mining the facts, readers analyse the situation by looking at the cause and effects, strengths and weaknesses, opportunities and threats presented in the case study. They develop their own decision criteria.

After they have understood the issues and options, readers would move into the final stage of analysis to recommend an option with clear justifications of their decision and develop a plan of action, if needed. At this stage, readers would also question their assumptions of the situation.

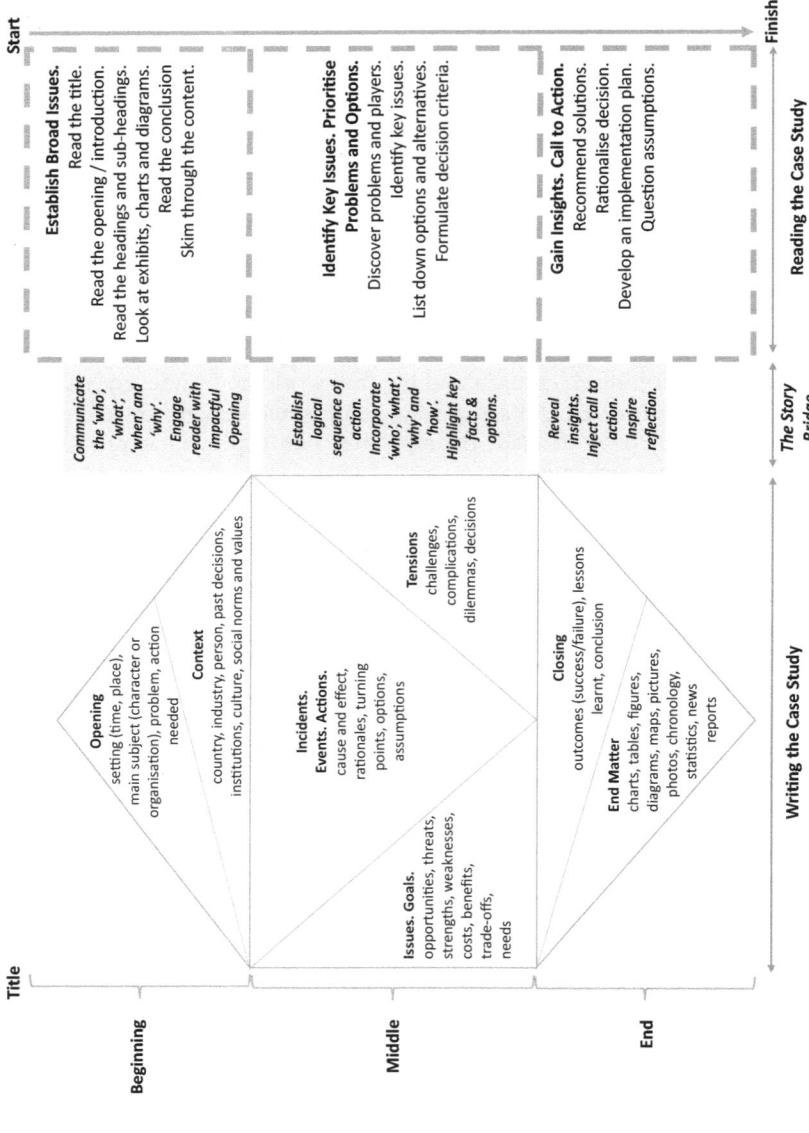

Fig. 5.2 Reading and writing the case study

Therefore, the End of the case study communicates the impact and implications of the points discussed and wraps up the discussion. Hopefully, by this time, readers will develop insights, new perspectives or experience a call to action as a result of their insights.

5.1.3   Story Bridge

The Story Bridge (Fig. 5.2) helps case writers to engineer the case study in such a way that it can draw on the reader psyche and make the case study relevant and reader-friendly. Therefore, in the Beginning segment of the case study, since readers are looking for clues to establish the broad issues of the case study, write an engaging Opening and embed the 'who', 'what', 'when' and 'why' into this first part of the case study. The goal is to capture the reader's attention and explain the purpose of the essay. To ensure that readers can establish broad issues easily during the first stage of their encounter with the case study, the title, introduction, conclusion, headings and sub-headings, and labelling of exhibits are critical to the case study structure.

In the Middle segment, events are described according to a logical sequence of action, highlighting the key facts and options. It contains information that explains and expands on the main issue. It elaborates and builds on the Beginning of the case study because readers start to read deeper to analyse the information presented in the case study. At this stage, they may consider the cause and effects, as well as the constraints and opportunities presented in the story.

For readers trained in management techniques, they would use tools such as PEST (political-economic-social-technology) and SWOT (strengths-weaknesses-opportunities- threats) to analyse issues.

Readers begin to identify the key issues and problems, prioritise problems, list down options and explore alternatives. As they do this, they also start to question if there is additional information that they need to help them make decisions about the issues presented in the case study. The five 'Ws' and one 'How' are also incorporated throughout the entire Middle. Explanations have to be clear and detailed because it is in the Middle that readers look for information to make their own analysis of the situation and develop recommendations. Tensions in this part of the case study keep readers engaged because they can identify with complications that occur in real situations.

Finally, the End segment re-affirms or debunks readers' own conclusions, and encourage reflection. Hence, the Story Bridge is a cognitive and emotive device.

The Beginning normally comprises roughly 10% of the case study, the Middle makes up around 80% and the End constitutes the remaining 10%. As case writer, your goal is to connect with readers, draw them into your story and keep them reading. Understanding the heuristic of readers affect how case studies are structured and written.

5.1.4   Three Basic Rules of Case Studies

The Case Jigsaw can be imprinted on any case study topic. It gives you a template for organising the content of your case study. To build your Case Jigsaw efficiently, follow these three rules.

a. Rule #1: Identify Key Takeaways

One of the first rules of developing form is not to give a blow-by-blow account of the event from beginning to end. First, this happened, then that happened, and this goes on until you get to the timeframe that you have decided to end the story. This only presents the situation in a straightforward manner, but it does not draw the reader to any specific angle, issue or problem that support the purpose of the case study. Your case study will only read like an entry in a diary or a page in history.

Similarly, do not construct your case study by simply putting together data from your sources. It should be more than a summary of the information that you have found. It must provoke thinking, analysis and questions. As you write each episode, constantly ask 'what are the key takeaways for readers?' at each juncture of the story and how do each of these small takeaways consolidate and lead readers to the penultimate lesson learnt at the end of the story. A case study should provoke readers to think, analyse, question and form their own opinions about what they had read.

Always organise the structure around the core points of the main idea, select the issues you want to highlight and incorporate the rationale, challenges, tensions and opportunities faced within each of these issues. Use your analysis during research to shape your case study. Look at the chronology of events, thematic clusters or data visualisation maps that you had created during the analysis of your research. Identify key turning points in the chronology and build a frame for the case study by creating headers for the key turning points. Under each of these headers, decide if you need to create another layer of sub-headers. Sometimes, you may choose to create a series of thematic sub-headers under each of the main headers. Once you have the headings and sub-headings, insert the cause and effects, assumptions, rationales, as well as the strengths and weaknesses of options and decisions, and weave in the tensions. When writing the case study, always build the story piece by piece, using each piece of the Case Jigsaw.

b. Rule #2: Connect Events and Actions

Organise information in a way that focuses the key issues. Enable readers to discover the key takeaways and sustain their interest from beginning to end. Using the storytelling principles of Campell's monomyth, Kenn Adams (2007) created an activity which he called *Once Upon a Time* to tell a story. This was later renamed the Story Spine by actor/trainer Kat Koppett[3] and used as a corporate-training technique.[4] Pixar's storytellers and story artists such as Andrew Stanton, Emma Coats and Brian McDonald have since adopted the Story Spine technique to develop narratives.[5]

This simple and popular technique makes use of six sequential trigger phrases:

- once upon a time ...
- every day ...
- but one day ...
- because of that ...
- until finally ...
- and every since then ...

These six phrases are triggers that force the case writer to think about how you want to order the action and express the key event in the action. The beauty of this storytelling technique is that you can grow the complexity of the story and weave in different milestones of development or weave in cause and effect of actions, layer by layer, in a structured way.

Some storytellers add a seventh trigger: the moral of the story. This can be done to highlight the lessons learnt from the event or incident. Although, if what you had written is engaging, meaningful and convincing, the moral of the story should have been implicit to readers. In fact, there may be many perspectives and multiple lessons that can be gained and not just what the case writer prescribes.

Tables 5.1 and 5.2 show two examples of how the Story Spine is used to build the Case Jigsaw.

Table 5.1   Constructing *The Wizard of Oz*

The Case Jigsaw	The Monomyth	The Story Spine	Events and actions
Beginning – Title – Opening – Context	Call to adventure (the start of transformation)	Once upon a time …	… there was a little girl named Dorothy who was carried by a tornado to the magical land of Oz.
		Every day …	… she journeyed towards the Emerald City in order to ask the Great and Powerful Wizard of Oz to help her get home.
		But, one day …	… she got to Oz and she met the Wizard.
Middle – Issues and goals – Incidents, events, actions – Tensions	Trials and victories (the process of transforming)	(1) Because of that …	… the Wizard told Dorothy that he would only help her get home if she killed the Wicked Witch of the West.
		(2) Because of that …	… Dorothy encountered many dangers
		(3) Because of that …	… the Wizard agreed to take Dorothy home in his hot-air balloon.
End – Closing – End matter	Return and re-integrations (revelation and transformation)	Until finally …	… on their day of departure, Dorothy ran after her dog, Toto, and missed the balloon.
		And ever since then, …	… Dorothy learned that she always had the power to get home on her own, which she did.

Source: Example of The Wizard of Oz story spine is reproduced with permission from Kenn Adams. Adams, Kenn. Back to the Story Spine. Aerogramme Writers' Studio, June, 5, 2013. http://www.aerogrammestudio.com/2013/06/05/back-to-the-story-spine/

Table 5.2 Constructing *The Incredibles*

The Case Jigsaw	The Monomyth	The Story Spine	Events and actions
Beginning – Title – Opening – Context	Call to adventure (the start of transformation)	Once upon a time …	… there was a superhero named Mr Incredible who was forced to live as an ordinary man in a society where superheroes were outlawed.
		Every day …	… he grew more and more frustrated with his stifling, boring life.
		But, one day …	… he accepted a secret superhero job from a mysterious stranger.
Middle – Issues and goals – Incidents, events, actions – Tensions	Trials and victories (the process of transforming)	(1) Because of that …	… he fell into the diabolical trap of this mysterious stranger who turned out to be Syndrome, a super villain with a long-time grudge against Mr Incredible.
		(2) Because of that …	… Syndrome was able to capture and imprison Mr Incredible.
		(3) Because of that …	… Syndrome could now take his master plan into motion by setting a giant, killer-robot loose on civilisation.
End – Closing – End matter	Return and re-integrations (revelation and transformation)	Until finally …	… Mr Incredible escaped from his prison and foiled the plan by destroying the giant, killer-robot.
		And ever since then, …	… he was loved by all and able to be a Superhero again.

Source: Example of The Incredibles story spine is reproduced with permission from Kenn Adams. Adams, Kenn. Back to the Story Spine. Aerogramme Writers' Studio, June, 5, 2013. http://www.aerogrammestudio.com/2013/06/05/back-to-the-story-spine/

c. Rule #3: Build Flexibility

When you write the Middle segment of the case study, revisit your case concept plan and remind yourself how your case study will be used. If your

Table 5.3 Two dimensions of case flexibility

Dimension	Degree of flexibility (1 is low while 3 is high)	Description
Adaptability	1	To re-write content significantly.
	2	To make slight modifications to the structure or content with minimal time and effort.
	3	To use the case study as it is with no re-arrangement of content or structure needed.
Modularity	1	To re-write content significantly.
	2	To re-organise content with minor re-writing with minimal time and effort.
	3	To add, delete or re-arrange entire sections quickly and easily without affecting other parts of the case study.

case study appears in a journal publication, then the case study will be an essay. However, if your case study is meant as an online resource that is part of a corporate learning material, you would need to structure your content into logical modules in consideration of user navigation. Or, your case study could have multiple uses where both the above possibilities apply.

The ease at which you can customise and package your case study for different purposes depends on two factors—its adaptability and modularity. Adaptability is the ability to use the existing case study in new environments or reshape it for new use or purpose with minimal time and resources. Modularity is the extent to which you can separate, add, remove or recombine parts of the case study to form a new story. Similar to the levels of difficulty (Chap. 3), the modularity and adaptability of a case study can be tiered into three levels (Table 5.3). Level 1 is the least flexible because the content cannot be easily re-used or extracted without major re-writing.

5.2   THE BEGINNING

5.2.1   Title

The title is the name of the story and the first signpost for readers. A descriptive title is straightforward and reveals the subject or theme of the case study in a concise manner. It is the expected title of academic works and research reports. A suggestive title uses catchy and creative words to hint at the topic of the case study. Suggestive titles are often used for fiction and narrative works.

Titles can be divided into two parts, separated by a colon or hyphen, to elaborate on the topic. The two-part title can also be a combination of descriptive and suggestive titles. Parenthesis and alphabets can also be used to show parts and sequence. Writing case study titles in a certain way can convey different messages to readers (Table 5.4).

Table 5.4   Examples of case study titles

Case study title	Comments
Supply Chain Hubs in Global Humanitarian Logistics[a]	This straightforward title describes the subject of the case study.
"Same Bed, Different Dreams": The China-Singapore Suzhou Industrial Park (A).[b]	This is a three-part title. The first part within quotations marks is the translation of a Chinese proverb. The second part describes the main subject of the case study. The third part in parenthesis denotes that this is a multi-part case study.
Turn the Ship Around! (A)[c]	Written with an exclamation mark, this title is provocative and commands the attention of readers. However, readers do not know the topic of the case study unless they read the case study. This is a case study about the United States Navy.
From Shadows to Sunshine to Shadows Again? Street Vendors and Their Struggle for Livelihood[d]	The title starts with a question to attract readers' attention by putting doubt in their minds. The second part of the title explains the subject matter of the case study.
Park Plaza (A)[e]	This title is the name of an area in Boston. It is only meaningful to readers who reside in Boston or are familiar with this project.

[a]Martinez, A.P, Wassenhove, L.V. and Stauffer, J.M. "Supply Chain Hubs in Global Humanitarian Logistics", 30 Jan 2017. https://cases.insead.edu/publishing/case?code=35736. Accessed on 21 Apr 2017

[b]Scott, E and Thomas, J. ""Same Bed, Different Dreams": The China-Singapore Suzhou Industrial Park (A)". Harvard Kennedy School Case Program. 13 March 2007. https://case.hks.harvard.edu/same-bed-different-dreams-the-china-singapore-suzhou-industrial-park-a/, accessed on 21 April 2017

[c]Hagen, Jan. U and Marquet, David. "Turn the Ship Around! (A)". ESMT European School of Management and Technology. February 20, 2017. http://www.thecasecentre.org/educators/products/view?id=142542, accessed on July 7, 2017

[d]Singh, Sudhir Pratap, Sinha, Shalini and Tapasvi, S.K. "From Shadows to Sunshine to Shadows Again? Street Vendors and Their Struggle for Livelihood". Asia Case Research Centre, The University of Hong Kong. 2016. Accessed on July 7, 2017 from http://www.acrc.hku.hk/case/free/16_574_1_17_3.pdf

[e]Diver, Colin. "Park Plaza (A)". Harvard Kennedy School Case Program. January 1, 1975. Accessed on July 7, 2017

5.2.2   Opening

The beginning of a case describes the focus and purpose of the case study. It situates readers and brings them quickly into the issue and topic. The angle and point of view which the case study will be told are also established.

More than just an introduction of the case study, the Opening must engage readers' interest and lead them into the rest of the content. Within the Opening, case writers must help readers answer these questions:

- What is the problem or issue?
- Where does the event take place? This refers to the geographical space, that is, the country, city, street or a specific physical location.
- When does the event take place? The time which the event took place could refer to the year, month or day. It could also refer to a span of time that lasts a few years.
- Who is the main character or which is the organisation involved?
- What are the needs and desires of the character or organisation?
- What is the action required?

Here is an example of an opening that begins with a quote to draw readers into the subject described in the case study. The angle of this case study is the sustainability of an arts school in Singapore.

Writing an Opening

"*When you think about the purposes of education, there are three. We're preparing kids for jobs. We're preparing them to be citizens. And we're teaching them to be human beings who can enjoy the deeper forms of beauty. The third is as important as the other two.*"
Tom Horne, state superintendent of public instruction, 2009[6]

Historically, the education system has been based on the study of words and numbers. The arts have a lower status than mathematics and science. However, arts education is valued for many reasons—it encourages originality, deepens sensibility, and promotes creativity. The arts connect people more deeply to the world and open minds to new ways of seeing.

Going beyond adding more arts in schools, the Committee on Specialised Arts School in 2004 recommended the development of an independent pre-tertiary arts school in Singapore. It wanted to identify, attract and groom young Singaporeans with interests and talents in the arts; raise the quality of entrants to tertiary arts, media and design programmes; and serve as a model of excellence for the arts and arts education. Arts observers and educators saw this as a significant development for the arts in the Singapore's education system because selection of students who enrol in the School would be based on both artistic talent and academic excellence.

The School of the Arts was the third independent specialised school to be set up after the establishment of specialised schools in sports (2004) and mathematics and science (2005). When the School opened in 2008, it received 1000 applicants for its inaugural intake although it had capacity for only 300, more than what the School had anticipated. In 2009, there were over 1000 applicants for 200 places. By end of 2009, the school had a total of 586 students. Some arts practitioners and educators had regarded the development of the School of the Arts as a coup within an education system that had been so deeply entrenched in economic excellence. This was a complete shift in mindset that the arts was only meant for under-achievers and placed it on par with other serious disciplines that emphasised reasoning and logic, such as mathematics and science. How can the School of the Arts influence education pathways and the eco-system to justify its relevance and existence in the long run?

Source: Author

5.2.3   Context

Context refers to the circumstances and conditions in which the issue occurs. It describes the place, time period, social norms and values, culture, institutions and structures, industry and state of affairs. It explains the environment in which the event took place. The context also provides the background by explaining past decisions, historical developments, constraints and paths taken previously. In fiction writing, this is known as the setting. In game design, this is the world in which the action takes place. Here is an example of how context of the Paris Métro was written in the case study on the Régie Autonome des Transports Parisiens (RATP). In order to understand the RATP, we would need to understand the history of the Paris and the Paris Métro.

Writing Context

The Paris métro is the second oldest métro in the world (1900), after the London Underground (1864). Although discussions and planning for the metro started as early as 1871, the decision to finally proceed with the construction was spurred by The Universal Exposition which was to be in Paris in 1900. The State had to build an underground rail system that could move high volume of visitors at the Exposition. The métro was developed during a period where Paris had been rejuvenated and transformed under the influence of Baron Haussmann. Haussmann improved safety, public health and traffic flow. He also built underground networks to remove waste water, supply fresh water and gas. Different parts of the city were designated for different purposes: the 17th district was peppered with stone houses for the well-to-do, green areas such as Gardens of the Champs-Elysées and Square de Trévise were added, and sites for a series of World Fairs were designated. Some called this the glory of the second empire and the World Fairs signalled the rebirth of France.

Source: June Gwee (March 2005). Art and Design as Strategic Management Tools. Thesis. Doctor of Philosophy in Visual Arts. Sydney: The University of Sydney.

If your case study is centred on an individual, an organisation or a country, then as part of context building, you will write about the person, organisation or country. Provide a concise description of the role, function, background, goals and needs of this entity. When the main subject is

Introducing Protagonist—Hector Guimard

Hector Guimard was in charge of the Art Nouveau entrances. Guimard was a neo-classic artist and architect. He was commissioned by the chairman of Compagnie du Métropolitain de Paris to create station entrances. He was given the brief to ensure that the entrances were environmentally friendly, complemented street communication and expressed the aesthetic trends and culture of that period. Guimard used art and design to achieve specific purposes for the entrances. He ensured that the entrance design was functional (commuters can use it as a visual marker to locate the entrance to the underground station), meaningful (expresses the values and attitudes of the city's leadership and vision), and a cultural symbol of the urban heritage of Paris (represents the art nouveau movement).

Source: Adapted from June Gwee (2008), *Art and Design for Strategic Management: Culture as Strategy*, Saarbrücken: VDM Verlag Dr. Müller

Introducing an Organisation—The RATP

The Régie Autonome des Transports Parisiens or RATP for short, was set up in 1948 as a public utility company with financial autonomy. It provided up to 75% of overall passenger traffic for public transport. It was a national company supervised by the government with the responsibility to operate all metro and bus lines formerly owned by the Compagnie du Métropolitain de Paris or CMP (Paris Metropolitan Railway Company) and the Office Regional des Transport Parisiens or ORTP (Public Transport Company of the Paris Région respectively. The RATP managed the Paris métro, Lines A & B of the RER (Regional Express Network) train system that ply the Greater Paris Area, the Paris bus network and the Paris tramway system.

Source: June Gwee (March 2005). Art and Design as Strategic Management Tools. Thesis. Doctor of Philosophy in Visual Arts. Sydney: The University of Sydney.

a person (also known as the protagonist), describe his/her education background, work experience, family, career, past achievements and failures and so on. The description connects readers with the protagonist and develops reader empathy for him/her. Here is an example of how you introduce a protagonist into a case study.

In the case study, the title, opening and context are sequential. However, you do not have to write them sequentially. Like a jigsaw, you can work on them independently first, then put them back-to-back when you are done. After you have joined them together, work in flow and link them together using specific words that connect one set of idea to another.

5.3   THE MIDDLE

The middle or body of a case study describes and establishes the plot of the story which comprises issues and goals; incidents, events and actions; and tensions. The plot refers to the events and action that gradually unfold for the reader. It organises the story, describing how people and events progressed from one state or condition to another within a specified time-frame. Progression and contrast are key concepts in all stories. They show the development of people and events from an existing state to a new state. The existing state could be a simple, general or positive state and the new state could be complex, specific and negative. Or, the existing state could be a negative situation and the new state an improved situation. It could also explain the cause and effect of actions.

5.3.1   *Issues and Goals*

This section elaborates and provides details of what was pre-empted in the Opening of the case study. The problem encountered could be complex, multi-faceted and contain several independent or inter-linked issues. Outline what these issues are and describe them in relation to the problem that needs to be solved. Sometimes, the problem highlighted in the case study could be a result of unmet needs or an outcome of specific goals. Explain these needs and goals, highlighting the opportunities, threats, strengths, weaknesses, trade-offs and benefits. When writing issues and goals, expand on both the protagonist or organisation, and the context, elements that you had introduced in the Beginning segment of the case study. You will notice from the example below that the organisation and context are interwoven into a single case study. The complex-

Writing Issues and Goals

La Caixa, one of Spain's largest savings banks with more than four thousand branches, 22,000 staff and a customer base of 8.6 million, wanted a corporate identity that reflected the bank's vision, personality and reputation. With a history dating back to 1904, la Caixa had been one of Spain's most respected organisations. Throughout its history, la Caixa had constantly transformed to stay relevant to its customers and the industry. New entities were formed while others were reconstituted.

In 2015, its vision was to build a better, more just society, that offered great opportunities to the people who most need them. The organisation's values were centred on social commitment, responsibility and confidence. How should the la Caixa brand reflect these values? Was its corporate logo, which was created in 1980, still relevant?

The la Caixa logo was created by Catalan artist Joan Miró. It consisted of a bubbly, twinkling star with the words 'la Caixa'. The five-point star in the identity symbolised enlightenment. The colours used in the design were based on the colours of the Catalan flag. Using the art of a Catalan artist as the corporate identity of the bank reaffirmed la Caixa's social and cultural responsibility to the people of Spain and the art of Catalan. Miró's art was whimsical, imaginative yet elegant and sophisticated. Adopting the symbol was an ambitious undertaking in 1980 that demonstrated the boldness of la Caixa as a financial institution. In contemporary Spain, la Caixa customer profiles had evolved. How do contemporary businesses and customers view the la Caixa brand? Would the original design of its corporate logo still reflect these values and the spirit of la Caixa? How can the design of this symbol continue to promote and advance the spirit of la Caixa, yet appeal to new customers?

Source: June Gwee (March 2005). Art and Design as Strategic Management Tools. Thesis. Doctor of Philosophy in Visual Arts. Sydney: The University of Sydney.

ity of this case study can be increased by adding in more context and issues.

5.3.2   *Incidents, Events, Actions*

Incidents, events and actions are described in detail. Discuss the cause and effect of actions, assumptions behind actions, options considered, rationales of decisions, availability of options and alternatives, and impact of outcomes. Explain the cause and effect of actions by highlighting the driving forces and intents of actions where possible. In the example below, the case study starts with action, that is, the collapse of the viaduct, and later reveals the cause of the collapse in the subsequent paragraph.

To put readers in the scene of the collapse, a descriptive writing style was used to recount the incident. Descriptive writing uses language and expressions that appeal to the senses. For example, '… toiled on to build the highway …' highlights how the workers worked hard on the construction of the highway, 'stunned' depicts the feeling of shock on the site while '60 civil defence officers' describes magnitude of the incident.

Writing Incidents, Events, Actions

In the early hours of July 14, as workers toiled on to build the highway along Upper Changi Road East, a horizontal portion of the viaduct gave way and crashed. Stunned, workers on the ground immediately rushed to look for their friends. There was a group of workers who were working on the structure when it collapsed.

The Civil Defence Force was called in and they arrived at the scene with K9 search dogs. Some 60 civil defence officers were involved in the search and rescue operation. One worker, who was on top of the structure when it collapsed, was killed. 10 others were also hurt as a result of the collapse. Authorities immediately issued stop-work orders. Preliminary investigations revealed that that corbels (brackets that supported the horizontal beams) had given way. Speculations by expert engineers pointed that human error might have triggered the collapse. Detailed investigations had been ordered to determine the cause of the collapse and prevent such incidents from happening in the future.

Source: Author

5.3.3 Tensions

Tensions are part and parcel of writing incidents, events, actions because life does not happen in a straight line in real world situations. Events are interrupted by unforeseen barriers which create a disequilibrium in situations and disrupt the flow of events. This is compounded because human behaviour is unpredictable and not always rational. Tensions are inevitably necessary in case studies because all organisations, industries and systems are created and managed by human beings. There will be unintended consequences and many moving parts with multiple players.

During child psychologist Édouard Claparéde's research on problem-solving in children, he found that disequilibrium creates a need in the child to act and try to restore the disequilibrium.[7] The work of developmental psychologist Jean Piaget's theory on disequilibrium also explained that the disruption to the individual's mental schema of things causes discomfort which motivates the individual to either adapt the existing schema or develop a new schema so that equilibrium can be restored.[8] Human beings have a natural tendency to want to resolve imbalances and resolve states of disequilibrium. Hence, readers naturally desire to correct the imbalance and restore equilibrium in the events that are being described. This is one of the main reasons why the description of tensions is one of the key ingredients of writing engaging case studies.

As case writers, we need to remember that readers have emotional and intellectual needs. Because of these fundamentals of what it means to be human, your case study will be interesting, compelling, meaningful and engaging to the target readers if it:

- contains tension and conflicts that readers can relate to,
- reveals how people changed or made things change,
- includes an element of surprise, twist or unexpected truths, and
- is topical.

There are different types of tensions that can cause disequilibrium. They could be man-made, a result of occurrences in nature or simply a systemic malfunction. I have outlined and described four types of tensions here: challenges, complications, conflicts and dilemmas (Fig. 5.3).

Fig. 5.3 Tensions that cause disequilibrium

Tensions can lead to turning points. These refer to critical incidents, radical changes or unexpected revelations that changes the direction of story. It can be in the form of a failure, an unexpected barrier, a change in leadership or an introduction of a new policy. Fiction writers call this device a plot twist. Turning points increase the tension of events and actions in the case study. They keep the narrative moving and anchored in reality. These shifts cause a change in readers' expectations. They can evoke feelings of discomfort, anger or betrayal in the reader which draw readers into the events described in the case study.

To engage readers, always describe the tensions in detail. Lead your readers into the tensions and developments rather than just listing down facts. When describing the incidents, events and actions, always reveal the tacit knowledge of the character and organisation by explaining the rationale of actions and decisions. Readers become immersed in the story when they can relate to the significance of actions, especially when the story appeals to both their heads and hearts. Use the 'show' rather than 'tell' technique (see Chap. 6, Sect. 6.2.6). Plan how you intend to guide them into these discoveries or series of discoveries. Then decide what information to put in, leave out, and where to put the information. This determines how your case study can be structured to achieve the compelling premise that you want to achieve.

The following example on writing tensions uses descriptive words such as 'tipped most likely to win' and 'demanded the criminal prosecution' to conjure strong feelings. Also, the technique of opposites such as 'denied vehemently to the charge but later apologised' shows a change of mind. The use of statistics—'100,000 protestors', '20,000 police officers' and '500,000 Muslims still gathered'—reveals the magnitude of the incident. The contrast of the first paragraph (where Basuki was tipped most likely to win) and the second paragraph (description of the change of events) also shows how the blasphemy charge was a turning point in this event.

Writing Tensions

In April 2017, Jakarta would elect a new Governor to serve a five-year term. The 2017 gubernatorial election was a much anticipated event for Jakarta residents. In September 2016, Basuki Tjahaja Purnama, announced that he would run for the Jakarta gubernatorial election. He was Deputy Governor of Jakarta from October 2012 to November 2014, and had been Governor of Jakarta since November 2014. Basuki wanted to continue his transformation of Jakarta and was tipped most likely to win the election despite being up against two strong candidates. Agus Harimurti Yudhoyono, the son of former Indonesian president Susilo Bambang Yudhoyono, and Anies Baswedan, former culture and education minister of President Jokowi's cabinet, were running against Basuki in the elections.

While on the campaign trail, Basuki was accused of blasphemy by the Indonesian Ulema Council for quoting from the Qur'an during a speech in the Thousand Islands. At first, Basuki denied vehemently to the charge but later apologised and said that he did not intend to offend anyone. However, his apology did not quell ground reactions that had already gained momentum. In November, 100,000 protestors from various Muslim organisations took to the streets in Jakarta and demanded the criminal prosecution of Basuki. Jakarta was placed on 'Siaga 1' alert, which was the highest security level. Even though 20,000 police officers were deployed to secure the city, hundreds were injured as a result of the demonstrations. On December 2,500,000 Muslims still gathered at the National Monument (Monas) Park in Jakarta and rallied for Basuki's arrest.

Source: Author. Compiled from media reports.

In short and compact case studies with single and specific events, there could be just one or two types of tensions. In case studies that trace a longer span of development or with multiple events happening at the same time, there could be more tensions and in different degrees.

These three pieces of a case study's Middle—Issues and Goals; Incidents, Events and Actions; and Tensions—are inter-linked. When you develop each of these pieces of your case study, you will find it hard to separate them. For example, as you write about an event that happened, you would inevitably have to describe the tensions and issues that surface during the occurrence of the event. Compared to the Beginning and the End, the Middle of the case study is the most challenging in terms of composition. To help determine the shape of your case study, first, identify key take-aways, then connect the events and actions, and finally, consider the flexibility of your case study for customisation.

5.4   The End

The end of a case study comprises the Closing and End Matter. By the time you reach this segment of your case study, you are either elated that you are at the finale or you find that you do not have energy to complete the last mile. Don't lose heart at this point because the Closing and End Matter are as important as the Opening and Context.

5.4.1   Closing

The Closing wraps up the case study. It can be a conclusion or a call to action for the reader. The most common type of Closing for a teaching case is to ask the reader 'what should the main character or organisation do?' This is a call to action and forces the reader to think of the next step. It also functions as a cliffhanger which puts readers in suspense and engages them to think about 'what next?'

Depending on the objectives of the case study, the Closing may include any or a combination of these elements:

- It reiterates the challenges today and in the future.
- It establishes a sense of urgency and importance regarding the issue surfaced in the teaching case.
- It qualifies the rationale and thinking behind certain choices and decisions.
- It assembles different aspects of the story into a single focal point.
- It inspires hope or creates despair.
- It describes and explains the lessons learnt.
- It presents new significance and/or applications.

Writing a Closing

By tracing the evolution of creative industries in Singapore, it can be seen that it took more than two decades for the creative cluster, including arts activities and related businesses, to gain sufficient visibility and credibility as an independent strategy for economic development, and as an enabler for innovation. Its rate of growth is slow compared to clusters in traditional industrial areas such as information technology and manufacturing. This may be characteristic of knowledge-based clusters with a high correlation to innovation as there is a limit to the rate which they can be accelerated without sacrificing organic growth.

The creative cluster of a small nation, such as Singapore, is an enabler for developing a national innovation system. The creative industries cluster strategy itself, although an economic strategy, is also the nation's innovation policy. Creativity through the arts cannot be divorced from the development of a smaller and younger nation even if its immediate goals appear solely economic. The notion of arts and local culture has to be taken seriously from the beginning and incorporated as early as possible through education, social and cultural policies because creativity, critical thinking competencies, and cultivating sensibilities for the aesthetics are dominant in the arts. These knowledge and skills become necessary as small nations move up the value chain to attain a more sophisticated level of competitive advantage for the economy and for the city as a whole. If these were not given importance from the beginning, as seen in this case study of Singapore, the smaller nation will find it considerably difficult to produce interesting and original content of a high standard when needed in the next phase of its development because it takes a decade for the results of education policy to be seen.

For a younger and smaller nation that needed to fast track its growth because of globalisation pressures, public policies that shape its social and economic development should reflect the complexities of industries within the creative cluster. The challenge for Singapore would be to sustain policies and incorporate them in a way so that they complement other policies within the larger system of public governance.

Source: Adapted from Gwee, June. 'Innovation and the creative industries cluster: A case study of Singapore's creative industries'. *Innovation: management, policy & practice*. eContent Management Pty Ltd (2009). 11: 240–252.

5.4.2   End Matter

Exhibits found at the end of the case study refer to all other supporting materials that are mentioned in the middle of the case study or which help readers better understand the issues and decisions described in the case study. They can also be information that supplements the narrative and are needed for a deeper understanding of the case study. These may include:

- Charts, tables, figures, diagrams, maps
- Pictures and photographs
- Chronology of events
- Newspaper clippings
- Statistics

NOTES

1. Campbell, Joseph (1949). *The Hero with a Thousand Faces*. Pantheon Books. p. 23.
2. Campbell, Joseph (1949). *The Hero with a Thousand Faces*. Pantheon Books. pp. 28–29.
3. Adams, Kenn. How to Improvise a Full-Length Play: The Art of Spontaneous Theater. New York: Allworth Press, 2007.
4. Koppett, Kat. Training to Imagine: Proper Improvisational Theatre Techniques for Trainers, Managers to Enhance Creativity, Teamwork, Leadership, and Learning. Stylus Publishing, 2012.
5. The Story Spine: Pixar's 4th Rule of Storytelling, 22 March 2013. https://www.aerogrammestudio.com/2013/03/22/the-story-spine-pixars-4th-rule-of-storytelling/.
6. Smith, Fran, "Why Arts Education is Crucial, and Who's Doing it Best", *Edutopia*, http://www.edutopia.org/arts-music-curriculum-child-development, date accessed: 26 Aug 2010.
7. Woodward, William R. Young Piaget Revisited: From the Grasp of Consciousness to Decalarge. *Genetic Psychology Monographs*. University of New Hampshire. Retrieved from https://philpapers.org/archive/WOOYPR.pdf.
8. Kiber, Jackie. Cognitive Disequilibrium. *Encyclopedia of Child Behaviour and Development*. pp. 380–380. Springer US. and Piaget, J. The Psychology of Intelligence. Routledge. May 17, 2001.

PART IV

Craft

CHAPTER 6

The Chronicler's Rune

The wordsmith is the artful imagineer, faithful to
the laws of language while sprinkling them with stardust.

Case writers are chroniclers. We record significant stories, facts and details of life distinctively and convincingly. A case writer's craft is a composite of style (S), linguistics (L) and voice (V), each of these three elements is independent yet inexplicably linked, to form a unique expression, or the writer's intellectual property. These concepts form the Chronicler's Rune (Fig. 6.1)—the case writer's skill in combining word choice, sentence construction, fluency of paragraphs, meaning conveyed in text, arrangement of thoughts and ideas, tone of voice, point of view, and choice of images and symbols to captivate the intellect, emotion and senses of readers. This is the case writer's craft. Cultivating craft requires great skill, considerable experience and endless practice.

A good case writer writes concisely, uses form and function to his/her advantage and knows how to vary style, voice and linguistics to suit different audiences and contexts. If you are writing the case study for a professional journal, then the writing style is one of authority. If you are

© The Author(s) 2018
J. Gwee, *The Case Writer's Toolkit*,
https://doi.org/10.1007/978-981-10-7173-7_6

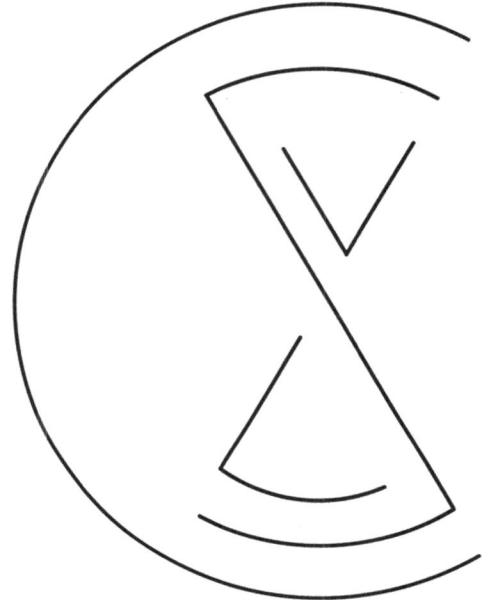

Fig. 6.1 The Chronicler's Rune

writing the same content but using it as a teaching case for undergraduate students, then the writing style changes to one that is more descriptive and vivid.

6.1   Writing Styles

Writing can be classified into four types of styles—narration, description, exposition and persuasion. Each of these styles possesses distinctive characteristics that set them apart from one another.

6.1.1   Narrative Style

A narrative is an account of people and connected events told in story form. The narrative form refers to the narrative structure of the case study while the narrative style refers to the style of writing. Using a narrative case structure, the writer tells the story by unfolding the events to readers. Readers comprehend, interpret and form their own views about the outcomes of the events.

Non-fiction writer and literary critic William Zinsser referred to the narrative as "the oldest and most compelling method of holding someone's attention: everyone wants to be told a story."[1] Simply because of human interest in stories, teaching cases are normally written in narrative form and narrative style so that students can put themselves in the shoes of the protagonist and immerse themselves in the issues and context presented in the teaching case.

The narrative style is storytelling. This is done by developing characters, setting, plot, action, conflicts and dialogue, similar to what we see in creative fiction such as novels, poems and movies. The case writer's opinion is absent in the narrative style. This style has also been used for non-fiction forms such as documentaries and autobiographies. It is a popular style because it can effectively transport readers and viewers into the world of the protagonist presented in the work.

According to Schaller and Tobin (2010), 'Narrative is a method whereby a story is crafted from events and the experiences of the writer, and refers to discourse that attempts to create understanding by telling a story that answers the question "what is going on here?" In this way narrative can contribute to the creation of understanding and knowledge in a more inviting manner for the intended audience.'[2]

For this reason, the narrative style is the predominant style of a narrative case study because it immerses learners in the shoes of the protagonist and the issues that he/she is faced with. The narrative style is excellent for narrative structures such as the monomyth, Freytag's Pyramid, the Story Wave and the Pinnate Venation (Chap. 7). These are ideal for writing case studies with themes on leadership and transformation because it reveals how people and events changed from one state to another, or from one condition to another.

The narrative style can also be used for knowledge-capture since it has been proven that stories are an effective way to engage readers and help them to remember messages and lessons. Similarly, the narrative style can also be used for research cases, especially if the research case mines for data through narrative inquiry or oral history approaches.

Narrative Writing Style

At Crossroads

During the early years, Ming-I was the sole designer cum account manager for all his clients. His company, Xander Graphics, was named after his only son, who was born the year that he registered his business. As his business grew, he started to employ graphics artists. Ming-I's scope of work was broad. He designed product labels, corporate logos, annual reports, wayfinding signages, posters, newsletters, book covers, advertisements, point-of-sale collaterals, storefront displays, food packaging and so on. Ming-I had a keen sense of client needs and relationship management. He was good at developing trust with those he worked with. His designs were bold and of high quality. The firm's design services came at a premium but he set trends and helped his clients re-define their businesses. Ming-I's design vision and business acumen helped land numerous acclaimed blue-chip projects and garnered international recognition for Xander Graphics.

On September 27, 2015, Ming-I finally handed over reins of the company to his son, Xander. After growing the business for 40 years, Ming-I was eager for his son to deepen his legacy in China. However, Xander thought that the domestic market was limited. He wanted to expand outside China and bring the brand overseas. He believed that the only way to grow the business was to acquire an international company with global networks. Ming-I strongly objected to Xander's idea because this would destroy the goodwill that he had built up with his clients in China.

Source: Author

6.1.2   Descriptive Style

The descriptive style visually presents people, places, events and actions in detail and through the use of metaphors, similes and symbols. Words are used to paint a picture. The descriptive style engages readers' senses of sight, smell, sound, touch and emotion. It is used in both fiction and non-fiction works because it adds realism and makes readers feel like they are placed in the midst of action. Like the narrative style, the descriptive style is also a popular writing style for teaching cases because it can immerse readers in a situation. To do this, write by showing readers what happened and unfold the events to readers rather than tell readers about the event.

The descriptive style works best in crisis-themed case studies because vivid and detailed descriptions are needed to reveal the vividness of actions, evoke feelings of urgency, anxiety, distress and present complexity of events. Because of the nature of this topic, readers can be brought into the story by using the descriptive style of writing. Imagery and words are used to draw readers into the crisis.

Descriptive Writing Style

Terror in the City

6 pm, Friday, November 20

It was six in the evening. Office workers poured out from the buildings, hurrying to the Central subway. Most did not know that the trains had stalled until they reached the platform. That was when they first heard the announcement that a bomb had exploded at Linden, just one station away from Central. There were gasps and people started to retreat from the platform back to the station entrance, hoping to exit Central. The air was thick with tension. The hurried footsteps quickly transformed into panicked runs towards the exit.

The station police had conducted emergency exercises for scenarios like these. Yet, their efforts to calm the crowd were futile. Their instructions to the crowd fell on deaf ears. The stampede that emerged rendered them helpless.

Source: Author

6.1.3   Expository Style

The expository style informs, explains and defines an issue, subject or topic. There is no character or plot development. Neither is there opinion. The expository style is concerned with only providing and explaining the facts—what it is, how things are done, what is the sequence of events. It is often used in scientific and technical writing.

The expository style can be used to write case studies on processes and systems where the storyline is sequential and straightforward. It can be used in writing teaching cases, research cases and knowledge-capture cases. However, because of its factual nature, it is less convincing in engaging readers and learners compared to the narrative and descriptive style, unless the target audience is in the same specialised and technical field.

Expository Writing Style

Deregulation of the Telecommunications Industry
A common pattern in deregulation throughout Asia was the liberalisation of the telecommunications industry. Regulatory bodies for telecommunications in Asian countries that were affected by this trend would invite local and international companies to tender for the provision of telecommunications services such as mobile communications, fixed-line communications, Internet access, value-added networks, international communications and so on. The conditions for the tender would be for several operators to compete for the same services or a combination of services within the same area or in different areas. It was a standard requirement by telecommunication regulators to expect the successful bidder of a telecommunication licence to publish a telephone directory and provide telephone subscriber information to the public.

The requirements of regulators varied from country to country. In more developed countries where information technology was dominant, for example, the European Union which had the EuroPages, subscriber information was available in both print and electronic form (compact discs, the Internet, Audiotex services). In developing countries with less adoption of information technology, traditional print medium dominated the scene.

Source: Adapted from Dennis Tan (1998), 'Developing A Strategy for a Telephone Directory Publisher Facing Deregulation. A Study of a Singapore Telephone Directory Publisher'.

6.1.4   Persuasive Style

The goal of the persuasive style is to convince readers to take the writer's position. The main differentiation of this style from the earlier three is that persuasive writing contains writer's opinions, arguments and justifications. Case studies that are submitted for journal publication may be written in persuasive style.

To persuade readers to take the position of the case article, writers use the three modes of persuasion—ethos, logos and pathos. Ethos asserts to readers that the case writer is trustworthy and credible. Logos appeals to the logic of readers by providing facts, delivering counter arguments, discussing alternatives and asking rhetorical questions. Pathos asks for readers' empathy, pity or anger, drawing upon their emotion to persuade them to the writer's position.

Persuasive Writing Style

Art and Design for Strategic Management
This is an era where innovation through knowledge, information and technology takes centre-stage. Since the invention of the computer, information technology has been ruling our lives in more ways than needed. We have allowed the Internet into our offices, our homes, our community and now, our minds; it has infiltrated every physical and emotional space that matters. Unwittingly, we are swept along by waves of change that these forces have generated. More disquieting is the extent of influence they will have on professions, businesses, governments, communities and individuals. The real question is how we will be transformed—the way we live, evolve and innovate. What is our future and who do we want to be?

The cyberspace is one of Man's greatest inventions where we have succeeded in playing God on our own turf and terms. It is also the beginning of the rapid deterioration of our only unique selling point—the human spirit. Our sensibility and sensitivity have diminished and human nature has remained stagnant. We are losing our humanity. The Internet has caused our social, psychological, emotional and sensory world to diminish into a computer screen. We now navigate news around the world, conduct business, keep in touch with friends and make new friends, without having to move away from our desk. Eager for recognition, our world seems to have broadened and our social sphere increased, but we remain lonely. Ironically, more and more people are reaching out, looking for new forms of engagement, seeking for meaningful experiences and taking on new personas in a different space as a way of escapism and finding a new source of adrenaline rush. We are still searching, but unlike the previous era, we are not seeking as consumers but as participants. It is not viable to use the same strategies to fight the wars of demand, supply, consumption, politics and power, notwithstanding that challenges brought about by increasing diversity, rapid globalisation, and relentless inequality are fragmenting society at a rate faster than ever. To have clarity of what really drives us and to rediscover the meaning in our routines, the seekers of the Internet age need a new saviour—culture.

Culture will remain in the chorus lines if it does not reclaim its purpose in a capitalistic world. Organisations are in the best position to achieve this because they are in the business of providing goods and services to the community, especially when the organisation provides a public good and service. They can exploit the benefits of culture to create value for the organisation and at the same time help it reclaim its glory through the holistic application of art and design within the organisation's strategic design management process. The critical question is: what does it take to cross into a state where art and design are the organisation's capital, where they are accepted and integrated as the organisation's strategic management process?

Organisations that deliver a public good or service are in a business where their destination is more social than commercial. It is about delivering the well-being of people where a cultural compass powered by art and design are formidable tools. They have the means to transform lives, reinforcing the identity of cities, changing the tune of businesses and redefining the notion of space. The pathway to the future converges into a single destiny—the ability to effectively use culture to create new identities, new space, new dreams, fresh hopes and new power.

The legacy of an organisation is its ability to return to humanity the fragments of soul that are lost as people become absorbed in their daily, mundane routines, powerless against larger forces that drive the economy and industry. Human beings interpret and process the world in non-rational ways where success and growth are states of mind. Attitudes and the search of meaning will drive choice and perception of value. The integration of art and design into the organisation's strategic management process reclaims the human spirit. Art as a strategic management tool is part of the organisation's language in creating sensitivity and sensibility. Design as a strategic management tool is a goal-oriented, process-based and holistic activity where systems thinking is used to define new perspectives for the organisation and its stakeholders so that new value can be created through the organisation's goods and services with the objective of generating new, useful and meaningful day-to-day living for the community.

This is an era where culture is the new capital within which art and design in the organisation are the instruments to revive the repertoire of public goods and services, and return meaning to lives. Man's labour under the sun is eventually about freedom of the heart and mind, about heritage, hope, well-being, imagination and a sense of wonder—the rudiments of meaning in life.

Source: extracted from June Gwee (2008), *Art and Design for Strategic Management: Culture as Strategy*, Saarbrücken: VDM Verlag Dr. Müller

6.2   LINGUISTICS

All case studies should be written in simple English. To achieve this, case writers must pay attention to sentence dynamics, active and passive voice, tenses, choice of words, spelling, punctuation and so on.

6.2.1   Sentence Dynamics

A sentence is a group of words that expresses a complete thought or a single idea. All sentences have a subject and a predicate. The subject performs the action described by the predicate, which is what is said about the subject. The predicate can comprise a verb (e.g. Dogs bark.), a verb and an adverb (e.g. The man walks slowly.), or a verb and the object which is the receiver of the action (e.g. Bruno won first prize.).

Some sentences are statements while others are questions (Table 6.1). They can also be commands, requests or exclamations. They can be manipulated to

Table 6.1   Types of sentences

Types of sentences	Examples
Statement	This is a dog.
Question	How are you?
Command	Be quiet.
Request	Please stand up.
Exclamation	Awesome!
Positive/affirmative	I am afraid.
Negative	I am not afraid.

sound positive or negative. Unless intended to achieve a certain effect, use positive sentences rather than negative ones to avoid confusing readers. Especially in topic sentences (i.e. the first sentence of a paragraph), use positive sentences to inform readers what will be discussed in the paragraph instead of what will not be discussed.

A simple sentence has a subject, verb and object. It contains a single idea and explains the relationship between the subject and the object. For example:

> Vivian [subject] is [verb] a doctor [object].

A simple sentence is different from a phrase which is constructed by combining a group or words to express an idea but do not form a complete sentence (Table 6.2). A phrase does not contain a subject and verb. Sometimes, a simple sentence is referred to as an independent clause because it can be used as part of a compound or complex sentence. A clause contains a subject and verb. Simple sentences are direct and best for clear communication. They are used to make important points.

A compound sentence adds details to a simple sentence. It is constructed by combining two simple sentences and joining them with a conjunction. It explains the relationship between the subject and object, as well as the cause and effect of the action in the sentence. A compound sentence helps readers see the value, reasons and justification of facts. It can also be formed by adding clauses to a simple sentence. For example:

> Avery practised hard and he became a famous pianist.

Table 6.2 Differences between clause and phrase

Types of sentences	Description	Examples
Sentence	Contains subject-verb agreement. Expresses a complete thought.	This is a dog.
Phrase	Does not contain subject and verb.	… around the corner
Independent clause	Contains a subject and verb. It is a complete thought and can be a standalone sentence.	… he became a famous pianist.
Dependent or subordinate clause	Supports a sentence and is not meaningful on its own.	… after much negotiation.

The advantage of a compound sentence is that it adds depth and richness to writing. However, if too many ideas are packed into a single sentence, this will confuse readers as they struggle to grasp the main point of the sentence. Nonetheless, compound sentences are still a useful literary device if you keep clauses simple.

Since a complex sentence contains multiple ideas, it contains an independent clause and one or more dependent clauses that explains the main sentence. A dependent clause is part of a sentence which on its own does not express a complete thought or idea, but supports the sentence to form the complete thought. Clauses can be arranged in a way to show cause and effect. For example:

> The old woman *[subject]* who lived in a tree-house built by her late husband *[phrase]* became *[verb]* homeless when the storm destroyed the house.

Dependent clauses help to indicate in a clearer and more specific manner the relationships of the subject, verb and object, which makes complex sentences very effective for explanations and descriptions. Again, like compound sentences, always balance between depth and clarity because readers will be confused if complex sentences are poorly constructed.

Where possible, use words rather than phrases and use phrases rather than clauses. Simple sentences work best for clear and direct communication. However, if a case study is written with only simple sentences, it will be a boring read because it lacks deeper explanations of relationships and rationales. Have a combination of simple, compound and complex sentences to create fluency of thoughts and ideas. They also add fluency and rhythm to the case study while reducing reader monotony.

6.2.2   Use of Conjunctions

Case writers sometimes wonder whether they should start a sentence with a conjunction, especially the conjunctions 'and', 'but', 'also', 'yet', 'or', 'so' and so on. These are known as coordinating conjunctions, and traditionally, they are used to join objects (e.g. 'I own a house and two cars.') or to join independent clauses (e.g. 'The soldiers were tired but happy to return home.')

Using a coordinating conjunction at the beginning of a sentence is done for several reasons:

- To create an emphasis:

  I do not believe in aliens. And I am convinced that they are a conspiracy.

- To contrast outcomes:

  They had issued many press releases on the event. Yet the media blamed the committee for poor communications.

- To create smooth transitions:

  Technology has disrupted industries. And it continues to pressure businesses to change their strategies.

Subordinating conjunctions such as 'when', 'as', 'whenever', 'if', 'since' and so on join the independent clause (e.g. 'When the company downsized, …') to the dependent clause (e.g. '… many executives became jobless.'). They are used in complex sentences for three main reasons:

- To transit between two ideas in the same sentence.
- To show the importance of the independent clause.
- To indicate times, place and cause-effect relationship.

For example:

- *After* the flash floods, the shopkeepers spent the day cleaning up their stores.
- Duncan expected to win the election *even though* he was late in campaigning for student council leadership.

The meaning of the sentence can be changed depending on where the conjunction is placed. For example:

- *Because* you smiled at me, I was happy all day.
- I was happy all day *because* you smiled at me.

In the first sentence, the emphasis is on the cause—the doer performing the action (smiling)—which brought about the effect (happiness) on the receiver of the action. In the second sentence, the effect (happiness) on the receiver is emphasised and the cause—the doer performing the action (smiling)—is the reason.

6.2.3   Active and Passive Voice

As much as possible, when constructing sentences, use the active voice instead of the passive voice. In active voice sentences, the subject performs the action described by the verb. In passive voice sentences, the subject is no longer performing the action but is acted upon by the verb. Sentences can be written in passive only if there is a direct object or if there is a doer and a receiver of action (Table 6.3).

In active voice, the subject or doer of the action is emphasised (i.e. Sally or the journalist). In passive voice, the object and receiver of action is emphasised (i.e. the media conference or the CEO). The organisation of the sentence between the doer and the receiver, and the subject and the indirect object, creates the cause and effect in the sentence.

Another reason that active voice is preferred is because there is always a doer of the action. When written in passive voice—'The company was restructured'—it does not say by whom. If it is written in active voice—'The CEO restructured the company'—it directly clarifies the subject/doer of the action. In passive voice, the relationship between doer and receiver of action is indirect which makes the reader work harder to understand the sentence. For clear and direct communication, use the active voice.

However, there is a place for passive voice. It is used:

- When the case writer does not know the doer of the action, or if the doer of the action is unknown or not needed in the sentence.

The votes were cast by mid-afternoon.

Table 6.3   Active and passive voice

	Subject-verb-direct object	Doer and receiver of action
Active voice	Sally organised the media conference.	The journalist interviewed the CEO.
Passive voice	The media conference was organised by Sally.	The CEO was interviewed by the journalist.

- To emphasise the action rather than the doer of the action.

The movie was downloaded a million times.

- For sentence variety and create fluency, flow and rhythm in the paragraphs.

There are indexes such as the Gunning Fog Index and the Flesch Reading Ease that measure readability. The Gunning Fog Index measures the average number of words in a sentence and the percentage of hard words that may cause the reader to stumble. The Flesch Reading Ease measures the length of a word and the length of a sentence. With practice, writers should aim to tell the most complicated story in the simplest way.

6.2.4   Tenses

A common dilemma for case writers is knowing when to use past and present tense. When writing case studies, keep to simple past, past perfect or future past tense for verbs (Table 6.4), unless the fact is a universal truth. This is because the case study describes an action or event that has already occurred.

A universal truth is a fact that is unchanging and constant. It applies to everyone and everything. Usually, universal truths refer to laws of nature.

Table 6.4 Forms of tenses

Types of tenses	Description	Examples
Simple past	Expresses an action that happened in the past.	He implemented the plan.
Past continuous	Expresses an action that happened before and after a given time in the past.	He was implementing the plan when the committee discovered the error.
Past perfect	Expresses an action completed in the past before something else happened.	The plan was implemented before the error was discovered.
Future in the past	Expresses an action that is expected to happen in the future from a time in the past.	The plan would be implemented.
Simple present tense	Expresses an action that is ongoing, or that which describes permanent situations, habits or routines, truths and fixed arrangements.	• The sun rises in the east. • Water boils at 100 degrees Celsius.

Table 6.5   Converting general truths from present to past tense

Present	Past
Elizabeth II is the Queen of England.	Elizabeth II had been the Queen of England since 1952.
Today, ABC Bank is the largest commercial bank in Asia.	In 2017, ABC Bank was the largest commercial back in Asia.
Seagate now has more than 46,000 employees worldwide.	Seagate had more than 46,000 employees worldwide in 2017.

For example, 'The sun rises in the east.' When describing facts that are universal truths, the simple present tense is used.

However, for general truths, it is better to write the fact in past perfect tense and add an adverb clause to qualify the reign (Table 6.5). This is because we do not know when readers will be reading the case study and if the facts that were general truths at the point of our writing will remain the same by the time they are read. These general truths are not laws of nature and they could change over time.

6.2.5   Headings and Paragraphs

A paragraph contains a single main idea. The ordering of paragraphs is also about ordering ideas. Begin each paragraph with a sentence that suggests the topic or with a sentence that helps with the transition of ideas. Paragraphs are used to structure and highlight key ideas so that readers can follow the logic of your ideas. Ideas should be developed within a paragraph or a section rather than placed as a list of bullet points. Bullet points are used to list items that do not require much elaboration.

Use different levels of heading to organise the content. Headings can be split into primary, secondary and tertiary level headings but avoid going beyond three levels because it will be difficult for readers to retain and process more than three levels of information. Each heading should contain a handful of paragraphs where each paragraph expresses a block of idea. Section headings should not contain just one block of text and ideas because this fragments the paper into ideas that are not substantially built upon.

6.2.6   Choice of Words

Write in clear English. Be concise and precise. Keep sentences short and avoid wordiness (Table 6.6). Delete redundancies unless you intend to use them for impact or to achieve certain outcomes.

Table 6.6 Avoid wordiness

Avoid	Use
in accordance to	according to
red in colour	red
round in shape	round
reached the conclusion	in conclusion
first of all	first
in a slow manner	slowly

Do not repeat the same idea by saying it differently because this will make your case study superfluous and rambling. Use active verbs and concrete nouns to avoid ambiguity. Do not have vague words or generalities such as 'world-class facility', 'excellent', 'unique', 'nice', 'state-of-the-art', 'breakthrough', 'very', 'quite', 'somewhat' and so on unless you are prepared to explain and elaborate what you mean; otherwise, these are meaningless to readers and they do not add to the point that you are making.

Reduce the use of jargon if you are writing to general readers. When using technical terms, concepts and scientific symbols, always explain or define them within the text or as footnotes to clarify them for readers. Once explained, the term or symbol used should mean the same thing and be referred to consistently throughout the case study. At the same time, be attentive to words and phrases that are over-used because they could reduce the significance of what you are trying to say and make your descriptions appear trite.

If you are writing the case study in an expository style, minimise the use of adverbs and adjectives. On the other hand, if you are using a descriptive and narrative style, include adverbs, adjectives, similes, metaphors and imagery to bring your words to life. These help to create a vivid and engaging experience for readers. Stay away from double negatives (e.g. I am not unaware) because they are indirect and tend to confuse readers more than achieve the dramatic effect that they are intended for.

6.2.7   Spelling

Words can be spelt in various ways. Among the many spelling styles, the two most distinctive styles are the spelling of American and British words (Table 6.7). Whichever style that you choose, always apply it to the entire case study for consistency.

Table 6.7   Selected word variants

American	British
analyze	analyse
center	centre
color	colour
defense	defence
organization	organisation
traveled	travelled

6.2.8   Abbreviations and Acronyms

Abbreviations are the short forms of words. They are used when terms and names are lengthy and they are repeated many times throughout the case study because you do not want to distract readers with the frequent mentions of the long term or name instead on focusing on the content of your case study. The abbreviation for the words 'for example' is 'e.g.' while 'ASAP' stands for 'as soon as possible'.

An initialism is a form of abbreviation. This is formed by the first letter of each word. NHL is the initialism for National Hockey League, while MRT is the initialism for Mass Rapid Transit. When an indefinite article is used in front of an abbreviation, always use the sound of the first letter to decide whether it should be 'a' or 'an'. Hence, the indefinite article for NHL is 'an' because NHL is pronounced as en-ehch-ell.

An acronym is also a form of abbreviation. It is a word that can be pronounced by combining the first few alphabets of each word in a phrase or name. UNICEF is the acronym for United Nations International Children's Emergency Fund while NASA is the acronym for National Aeronautics and Space Administration. At the first mention of the term or name, always spell it in its long form with its abbreviation in brackets.

6.2.9   'Show' and 'Tell'

A common advice for writers is to show, not tell. What this refers to is the use of words and sentence structure to change the way readers experience what you convey to them. In writing, to 'show' is to describe events and incidents in the story by immersing readers in the action. In other words, to 'show' involves readers in the experience, to see from the point of view of the protagonist. To 'tell' is to relate an event or action to readers using third person perspective or passive voice. This technique detaches the

Table 6.8 Show versus tell

Show	*Tell*
Immediately, she answered that the refunds were not allowed for sale items.	She had to think quickly in order to explain why the customer should not be given a refund.
His hands were like ice.	It was cold.
'That is not good enough!' the CEO snapped.	'That is not good enough!' the CEO replied angrily.
The winds pounded on the city, leaving a trail of overturned cars, fallen street lamps and shattered glass.	The city experienced strong winds because of the typhoon.

reader from the action which, at times, also slows down the pace of action that is being described. In 'tell', the case writer's voice is stronger.

It is not always true that all writing must be 'show', and not 'tell'. It depends on the goal of your case study and the intended effect of your writing on your reader. If your case study is expository or persuasive with a lot of explanations for a technical reader, then it is more suitable to adopt a 'tell' technique where you inform readers. On the other hand, if you are writing a narrative or descriptive case study with plot, characters and lots of action, then the 'show' technique may be more suitable because you want to evoke emotions and appeal to their five senses.

To help you better understand the difference between 'show' and 'tell', here are some examples (Table 6.8). You will notice that 'show' sentences create vivid mental images and evoke strong emotions.

6.2.10   Punctuation

Punctuation refers to the symbols that are used in the construction of sentences. There are basic rules to punctuation:

- Start a sentence with a capital letter (e.g. The cat jumped into her arms.)
- End a sentence with a full stop (e.g. Spring has arrived.)
- Use the comma to separate a list of words (e.g. I bought sugar, salt and butter.)
- End a question with a question mark (e.g. Who is that man?)
- Use the apostrophe to show possession (e.g. Pauline's watch is spoilt.)
- Use capital letters for proper nouns (e.g. Tokyo, Andrew, Samsung)

- Hyphenate compound words (e.g. chief-of-staff)
- Insert a comma before the conjunction in a compound sentence to separate the independent clause (e.g. Her circumstance was hopeless, but she might have one more chance to turn things around.)

Ensure that punctuation is correctly used or the meaning of the sentence may be changed. For example:

1. When he spoke French, girls were hypnotised.
2. When he spoke, French girls were hypnotised.

Most house styles stipulate that numbers one to nine should be spelt out in words while numbers from 10 onwards can be depicted in their numeric form. If numbers appear at the beginning of a sentence, they should also be spelt out in full and the first alphabet is capitalised as in a standard sentence.

Likewise, when the word 'percent' appears as part of a sentence, this is spelt out. When it appears in tables as part of statistical information, the symbol '%' is used. However, this again depends on the nature of your case study and the preferred house style of your institution. For example, in a financial case study which describes the dilemmas of mergers and acquisitions, it could be filled with numbers and statistics. In such a situation, you may decide to use the symbol '%' within the text of the narrative so that it is more reader-friendly.

6.2.11   Point of View

The point of view of a case study refers to the perspective which the case study is written. Stories can be written from three basic point of views: first person, second person and third person (Table 6.9).

Table 6.9   Points of view

Point of view	Pronoun used
first person	I, we
second person	you
third person	he, she, it
third person limited omniscient	Only one person (he, she or it) is used
third person omniscient	More than one person (he, she or it) is used

The third person point of view is used for case studies because it allows case writers and readers to be privy to the information presented. People, organisations and committees are referred to as 'he', 'she', 'it', 'they', 'him', 'her', 'them' and so on.

If the case study has a main character and the narrative is told from the point of view of the main character, then the writer describes the issues, actions and feelings from that character's perspective. This is known as third person limited omniscient point of view. This way, readers are transported to the context and experience of the character and his world created in the case study.

Alternatively, the case writer could also use a third person omniscient point of view to present a balanced description of a real event by presenting perspectives of different characters who were involved in the issue. This is the advantage of the third person point of view. Another advantage is that it allows case writers to present descriptions and opinions that are independent of the case writer's personal views since the case study is meant to be an objective account based on facts.

However, writing in the third person omniscient point of view is challenging because case writers have to ensure that the voices of characters in the case study are distinct enough for readers to differentiate between perspectives. Case writers must also guard against switching points of view too often because this will diffuse the flow of the story. Often, case writers who have a strong writer's voice find themselves writing their personal point of views and comments into the case study instead of presenting the views of the characters.

6.3   Voice

A writer's work reveals the writer. The case writer's voice refers to a combination of the his/her attitude (values and beliefs) and personality (e.g. positive, negative, cynical). It refers to how case writers use tone and language to present the facts.

A case writer's voice can be informal (chatty, conversational, casual, fun and impersonal) or formal (authoritative, professional, objective, serious and reflective). Other times, the case writer's voice can be passionate, humorous, sad, anxious, excited or whiny. Asking for a cup of coffee can be done in many ways—it can be as simple as 'May I have a cup of coffee?' or 'Don't you serve coffee here?'

There is a strong tendency for case writers to write the way they talk. This may or may not be good for the case study. It depends on the subject matter, the target readers, the purpose of the case study and the context of the case study. For example, if you are writing an official document that will be read in a formal setting, then the case writer may choose to use a reserved and decorous voice. But if you are writing for a contemporary audience and your writing goes into a social media platform, then your voice should be one that is informal, persuasive and conversational.

Just like how we speak differently in different situations, case writers should also be versatile in developing different types for voice for different readers and contexts. In case writing, because we are specific about the purpose of our case studies and our target readers, case writers have relatively less flexibility than fiction writers to cultivate their own distinct voice. Also, it is not easy for writers to develop a distinct voice, this comes with practice and exposure to different types of writings. However, over time, if you write case studies long enough, don't be surprised if you may find that friends start to recognise your writing without reading your byline. This, then, is evidence that your distinct writer's voice has emerged.

6.4   Intellectual Property

The intellectual property or copyright of case studies usually resides with case writers and/or with their organisations. If case writers are providing a writing service for which they are paid for then the case study belongs to the commissioning entity. Ownership of intellectual property should be clarified at the start of the project to avoid ambiguities and discrepancies during the case development process. Copyright also means that besides the copyright owner, no one else should have the authority to change anything in the case or the way that it is presented.

6.4.1   Citations and Footnotes

A citation acknowledges and attributes the source of the materials used in the case study. Citations can refer to published or unpublished materials and appear as footnotes or endnotes. They tell readers about the work by listing the:

- Name of author and co-author/s
- Name of interviewer

- Name of respondent
- Title of the works
- Name and location of the publisher
- Date of publication
- Date of interview
- Page numbers, if the work is a segment of a longer publication
- Weblinks, if the work is retrieved from the Internet
- Date when the work is accessed online

Citations give credibility and accuracy to the case study, especially for research and knowledge-capture case studies where evidence-based information is important to readers, who may comprise subject matter experts, industry veterans and stakeholders who participated in the research of the case study.

Citations, although equally important for teaching cases, are less emphasised because the teaching case is an instrument of the case method where it supports case discussions and pedagogy, rather than used as a research product. In some instances, a teaching case that is peppered with numerous citations and references may distract learners and prevent them from immersing themselves in the world described by the teaching case.

From experience, it is always better to over-cite than under-cite when writing the initial drafts simply because it is easier to delete citations than add them at a later stage. With a well-cited paper, case writers can always re-visit the facts and sources of information when re-writing and editing the case study. The citations are also useful for reviewers when they verify the accuracy of information. You can always choose to reduce the number of citations before the case study is published or formatted for use as a teaching case. Then, you also have the option to transfer some of the citations into the teaching note or place them in the bibliography.

Some commonly used citation styles are the APA (American Psychological Association), MLA (Modern Language Association), Harvard referencing and The Chicago Manual of Style which specify consistent formats in organising information. For more information and examples of other style guides, visit their respective websites for the latest updates. Publishers and organisations have preferred style preferences which may incorporate one of the abovementioned styles into a house style for their publications. For example, a house style that incorporates APA style guide could look like this[3]:

Book
One Author
Gwee, J. (1995). The great planet adventure. Singapore: EPB Publishers.
Editor
Gwee, J. (2012). (ed.). (2012). Case studies in public governance: building institutions.
Oxon: Routledge.
Chapter or Part of a Book
Neo B. S., Gwee, J. and Mak, Candy. (2012) Growing a City in a Garden. In J. Gwee (Ed),
Case studies in public governance: building institutions (pp. 11–63). Oxon: Routledge.

Newspaper/Magazine/Journal Article
Gwee, J. (2014, December 17). Innovation and the creative industries cluster: A case study
of Singapore's creative industries. *Innovation: Organization and Management.* 240–252.

Websites
United Nations Educational, Scientific and Cultural Organization. (n.d.) About the
educational sector. Retrieved May 22, 2017 from http://en.unesco.org/themes/
education-21st-century/about-us

Interviews
Tan, D. (2015, November 9). Interview by J. Gwee [In person].

Sometimes, supporting information or disciplines are provided as footnotes or endnotes. To minimise the use of footnotes for explanations or definitions, which could interrupt readers' flow of thought, integrate the ideas
into the main text or evaluate if the additional information is really necessary.

6.4.2   Disclaimers

Teaching cases must have a copyright statement and disclaimer either on
the front or back page. If the case study is disguised, this should also be
included in the disclaimer.

A typical copyright statement would look like this:

[NAME OF AUTHOR/S] prepared this case based on primary and
public sources. This case is intended for class discussion and learning, and not intended as source research material or as illustration of
effective or ineffective management. The names of individuals and
organisations in the case study have been disguised
COPYRIGHT ©2017 [NAME OF ORGANISATION]. All rights
reserved. No part of this publication may be copied, stored, trans-
mitted, altered, reproduced or distributed in any form or medium
whatsoever without the written content of both parties.

6.4.3   Permissions

The case writer must obtain formal permission from the participating organisation or individual before using the case study. Permissions can be obtained by getting the individuals or representatives of the participating organisation to sign a release form. The release form verifies that the information presented in the teaching case is authentic and accurate at that point of time. The release form also gives the case writer permission to use and publish the case.

There are six different types of information releases:

a. **Standard Release**

The most common type of release is to allow unrestricted use of the case study for educational and non-commercial purposes. If the case writer assigns publishing rights to a publisher, then the publisher of the case study can grant others the right to use the case.

b. **Restricted Release**

A restricted release allows the case study to be used by only the case author, for a specific purpose, or within a specific institution. It restricts use in other situations. Some organisations choose to limit distribution of the case study for business or strategic reasons.

c. **Multiple Release**

Multiple release occurs when a case study involves many organisations or interest groups. In such instances, multiple sign-offs may be required where two or more release forms accompany a single case.

d. **Delayed Release**

Occasionally, a case study may contain sensitive information or information that may affect company operations. Here, the organisation or individual can request a delay in distributing and publishing the case until a specified amount of time has passed or on condition that the case study will not to be used before a certain date.

e. **Re-release**

When a case writer makes substantive changes to an existing case, a re-release for the case study may be needed. Content changes, as well as the way words are phrased may affect the way the organisation and individual are perceived by readers. Hence, a re-release is required to request for permission to use the revised case study.

f. Release Not Required

Case studies written from public records do not require a release. Although a formal release is not required, sometimes, in the interest of maintaining good relations and professional practice, case writers may still choose to send the case study to the organisation or individual as a gesture of courtesy and for goodwill.

Case writers should consult their lawyers or legal departments before formalising the release form Table 6.10 and Table 6.11 show two samples of release forms which you adapt to create your own release forms.

Table 6.10 Release form for organisations

[Date]
Case Study Information Release Form
Permission is granted to _____ [name of case writer or the case writer's organisation] to use the information provided by _____ [name of the organisation granting the release] for writing, publishing and distributing (for educational and training purposes) the case study specified below.

Case Study Title:	
Serial Number:	
Case Study Author/s:	

This case is released in its original form.

Name:	
Designation:	
Organisation:	
Address:	
Signature:	

Table 6.11   Release form for individuals

[Date]
Case Study Information Release Form
Permission is granted to _____ [name of case writer or the case writer's organisation] to use the information provided by _____ [name of the individual granting the release] for writing, publishing and distributing (for educational and training purposes) the case study specified below.

Case Study Title:	
Serial Number:	
Case Study Author/s:	

This case is released in its original form.

Name:	
Address:	
Signature:	

NOTES

1. Zinsser, William (2001). *On Writing Well: The Classic Guide to Writing Non-Fiction.* First Harper Resource Quill. p. 62.
2. Schaller, P. & Tobin, K. (2010), Quality control and the genres of qualitative research in P.C. Taylor, K. Tobin & P. Gilmer (eds), *Sunflowers: the blooming of college and university education.* Hillsdale, NJ: Lawrence Erlbaum. p. 40.
3. American Psychological Association. *APA Style.* Accessed from http://www.apastyle.org/ on May 21, 2017.

PART V

Composition

CHAPTER 7

Writing the Case Study

Stories never die, they live forever.

Now that you are equipped with the case writer's tools, you are ready to write your case study. The design of the case study is determined by the subject matter and the purpose of the case study. Here are examples of common types of case studies to show you how form, function and craft are combined. Each of these case studies has specific features which you can adopt when you write for your own writing.

7.1 THE PROCESS CASE STUDY

A process case study describes the series of steps taken to achieve a specific objective. The steps are generally sequential and the writing style used is often expository in nature which focuses on telling and explaining how things are done. Hence, the story often happens in a straight line where events move from an existing state to a new state (Fig. 7.1).

Because sequence and phases of development are important in a process case study, the structure of this type of case study contains headings that coincide with the steps of the process. This is a logical way of organising and structuring the case study because the objective is to help readers understand how things were done at each phase and the considerations at every juncture.

© The Author(s) 2018
J. Gwee, *The Case Writer's Toolkit*,
https://doi.org/10.1007/978-981-10-7173-7_7

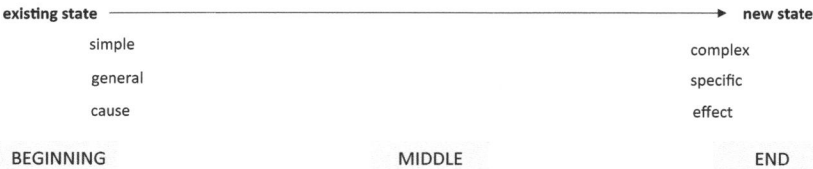

existing state ————————————————————————▶ new state

simple   complex
general   specific
cause   effect

BEGINNING   MIDDLE   END

Fig. 7.1   The Story Line

Process Case Study

Strategic Design Management
From 2000 to 2015, Ixora Channel had been providing urban planning solutions to cities. One of Ixora Channel's strengths was in town planning. As part of town planning, the organisation's design strategies were accorded the same level of importance as any other core functions such as human resource, finance, sales and marketing, and operations. The design management department managed all aspects of the design development and implementation. This department reported directly to the chief executive officer of Ixora Channel.

The design management department performed four main functions: establish the design code of practice, determine the approach for carrying out design practice, outline communication strategies that champion design, and audit design practices.

The strategic design management process in Ixora Channel was an iterative process that starts with identifying the problem before developing the conceptual framework and implementing it. During and after implementation, Ixora Channel would carry out after action reviews to identify the successes, failures, challenges, and lessons learnt during the project. The results of the review were re-channelled into the project as either new problems or a refinement of existing issues and goes through the same cycle.

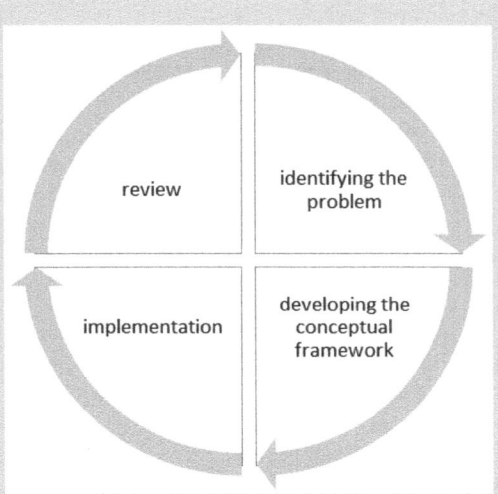

Step 1: Identifying the Problem

First, the project team would understand the issue by emphasising on asking questions and not be pre-occupied with aesthetic and stylistic expressions. Once the issue was clear, the manager defined the conceptual frameworks to prioritise the problem—thinking about why the project team should be concerned with the issue, what was it for, what was its intent and what should be done about it. Often, the questions asked had no immediate answers and required new investigations and new ways of viewing the issue. The aim was to strive for holistic, long-term solutions and not solutions that were based on short-term gains or individual preferences of decision-makers.

Step 2: Developing the Conceptual Framework

Next, the project team would translate the conceptual frameworks into actual, tangible solutions. This involved defining needs (i.e. who is it for, how to do it, how would customers behave and so on), perceiving things differently (i.e. can the same idea that was used in the past create a different response), reflecting on the rationale, and developing the technical requirements needed to implement the solution.

Step 3: Implementation

The project team would implement the plan by taking into account the control procedures, quality, cost, time and other related issues. The team undertook the responsibility of design and production, and oversaw the project from start to finish. No parts of the project were outsourced or passed to another unit in the organisation. This way, the project team would gain knowledge and experience on how to improve and implement future projects better.

Step 4: Review

After each project had been implemented, the team would gather to reflect and discuss their experience working on the project. During this meeting, the team highlighted what they thought went well and what they believed could have been done better. The issues and problems that remained unsolved were flagged out and identified as ideas for improvement using the design management cycle. This way, Ixora Channel used the design as both a strategic design management tool for projects as well as a learning tool for organisational learning.

Ixora Channel emphasised clarity in the design vision for each town planning project. The vision for the project had to be aligned to the design philosophy of the organisation which guided the policies and standards for each town design project. The design philosophy was incorporated into every function of the organisation, including its operations and day-to-day activities. Because of its design philosophy and principles, Ixora Channel was careful in accepting projects.

The design management department had developed a design charter that described the design practices in Ixora Channel. The charter also cemented the importance of the design management as a strategic function in the organisation. These components of the design charter guided the design management process and all design projects:

- [social value] represent the identity and heritage of a community of people
- [aesthetic value] communicate sensitivity and sensibility through style and form
- [functional value] deliver utility and performance

- [urban value] convey the planning, development, quality and living conditions in the city
- [intellectual value] incite knowledge, understanding and meaning
- [emotional value] evoke feelings of belonging and relationship

Since 2012, the organisation only accepted projects from companies whose mission and values were aligned to Ixora Channel's design philosophy. This limited the business growth but made Ixora Channel a niche urban solutions specialist in the industry.

Source: Author. This case study excerpt was written from secondary sources. The names in this case study have been disguised.

Process case studies tend to be factual and technical. To make it a more compelling read, try to include visuals, charts and diagrams to help readers better understand the process. These will also support the descriptions that you have outlined in the text. In terms of telling a process story, avoid embellishing it with descriptive language for the sake of making the case study engaging. This will make the case study over-dramatic and reduce the credibility of both the case content and the case writer.

7.2   THE ETHICS CASE STUDY

An ethics case study describes an ethical dilemma confronting a main character who has to make a decision. There are generally no clear-cut solutions because of the moral principles and values that are akin to the main character or protagonist. One way to present an ethics case is to end it with a dilemma or cliffhanger and leave the reader to decide what the protagonist should do. Alternatively, you can tell the full story with the climax in the middle of the story and describe what was the consequence of the protagonist's action.

This type of story form follows Gustav Freytag's story pyramid. Gustav Freytag (1863) had analysed five-act plays and stated that stories comprised five basic stages of action: exposition (setting the scene), rising action (building tension), climax (highest point of tension, usually a turning point), falling action (declining tension as conflict unravels) and denouement (resolution as the action ends).[1] If you end the case study with a cliffhanger, then you are using only the first half of Freytag's pyramid. If you tell the full story with cause and effect, then your case study forms a complete pyramid.

Here is an example of an ethics case study ending with a single peak. It can be extended to include a resolution or continued into another set of peak and trough.

Ethics Case Study

At Crossroads

Xander Wei is one of China's second-generation entrepreneurs who are taking over family businesses. After graduating with an MBA from Harvard University, he returned home to take over his dying father's design firm, Xander Graphics. Despite his western education, Xander considered filial piety a key Chinese virtue—children have a duty to their parents. They must respect their parents, be good to their parents, take care of their parents, bring a good name to their parents and ancestors. As the male heir of the family, he also has a duty to honour his father's will.

Xander Graphics

Xander Graphics was started by Ming-I Wei in 1985. He named the company Xander Graphics, after his only son who was born that same year. From the beginning, Ming-I had intended to hand the business to his son. Ming-I was a graduate from the Central Academy of Fine Arts, one of Asia's leading art schools. During the early years, Ming-I was the sole designer cum account manager for all his clients. As his business grew, he started to employ graphics artists. Ming-I's scope of work was broad. He designed product labels, corporate logos, annual reports, wayfinding signages, posters, newsletters, book covers, advertisements, point-of-sale collaterals, storefront displays, food packaging and so on. Ming-I had a keen sense of client management. He was good at developing trust with those he worked with. His designs were bold and of high quality. The firm's design services came at a premium but he set trends and helped his clients re-define their businesses.

Business Strategy & Culture

Ming-I's strategy was two-fold: look for new business, and retain existing clients to sell them new solutions. The new clients helped grow Xander Graphic's topline while the existing clients prevented the erosion of current revenue stream. To sell new services to existing clients, Xander Graphics would constantly engage them, thinking about their business issues, solving their problems, and keeping a close tab on their clients' industries. Account managers in Xander Graphics spent a considerable amount of time building trust and advising clients so that Xander Graphics remained their first point of contact. Sometimes, account managers would compile data analytics reports for their clients to keep the communication channel warm. This had been the culture in Xander Graphics for 40 years. Ming-I's design vision and business acumen helped land numerous acclaimed blue-chip projects and garnered international recognition for Xander Graphics.

On September 27, 2015, strickened with cancer, Ming-I finally handed over reins of the company to his son. After growing the business for 40 years, Ming-I was eager for his son to deepen his legacy in China. However, Xander thought that the domestic market was limited. He wanted to expand outside China and bring the brand overseas. He believed that the only way to grow the business was to acquire an international company with global networks. Ming-I strongly objected to Xander's idea because this would destroy the good will that he had built up with his clients in China. On his death bed, Ming-I made Xander promise to keep the business in the family and pass it down to the third generation of the Wei family.

In 2017, two years after his father's death, the firm's profits plunged by 60%. Xander Graphics had focused on higher billable hours, and account managers spent less and less time with their clients. Relationships became transactional because time spent with clients were billable. Account managers were overloaded with projects and the extra time spent with any client outside of the immediate project was an opportunity cost.

Xander re-examined the firm's business strategy. He knew that there were two ways that revenues could increase: increase the number of employees or increase the hourly rates billed to clients. He still believed that he needed to expand outside China and bring the firm's brand overseas. As he contemplated his options, a large multinational advertising corporation offered to acquire Xander Graphics which would solve the firm's revenue problems. With the acquisition, Xander Graphics would lose its brand name but all its employees would be absorbed into the MNC. Xander Graphics had a staff strength of 25 employees, 80% of which were staff who had been with the company for 20 years.

Xander had promised his father that he would keep the business in China and safeguard the company for the third generation of the Wei family. But if he did not take this opportunity with the MNC, Xander Graphics might not stay afloat for long. What should Xander do?

Source: Author. This case study excerpt was written from secondary sources. The names in this case study have been disguised.

Ethics cases are sometimes referred to as vignettes because they are only one or two pages long. A vignette case study is a brief story to illustrate a specific theory, idea, episode or dilemma. Vignettes can also be cast as a scenario that describes an evocative dilemma for readers or learners to solve. Vignettes can appear as a box story within the main case study or it can be a write-up on its own. A box story is a brief side story outlined by a box and placed within the main story, usually next to the text of the main story where the topic of the box story is mentioned. Due to its length, vignettes do not contain in-depth developments of character, plot or context. They zoom in on the person, issue or problem to give a powerful, and hopefully, lasting impression.

7.3   THE STRATEGY CASE STUDY

A strategy case is a case study that describes an entity's plan of action to mobilise resources, using knowledge of the environment, to achieve specific goals. The entity can be an organisation, a committee, a country or an individual. Strategy cases describe actions and events related to strategy development, strategic management, and operations. Very often, these cases also explore related themes such as leadership, transformation and innovation. There is a tendency for strategy cases to be more complex compared to process and ethics cases. This is because understanding the impact, cause and effect, and drivers of strategy requires broader and deeper descriptions about the context of strategy development and implementation, as well as explanations about the rationale, criteria, considerations, and deliberations that are associated with every decision.

This becomes more complicated because in real world situations, things and events do not occur in a straight forward manner nor do they have only a single turning point. Hence, the Story Line and Freytag Pyramid may not fully depict the complexity of people and events. An alternative to the Story Line and Freytag Pyramid is the Story Wave. A story wave is a story structure where there are multiple rising and falling actions as well as turning points (Fig. 7.2).

These varying levels of peaks and troughs are the complications and plot twists that occur during different points of time. The peaks and troughs have varying heights because there are different degrees of tensions and disappointments, some more severe while others minor. These different levels help the case writers to vary their emphasis of the event, activity or incident that they are describing, and calibrate the voice, tone and style of their writing. The story wave also helps case writers decide

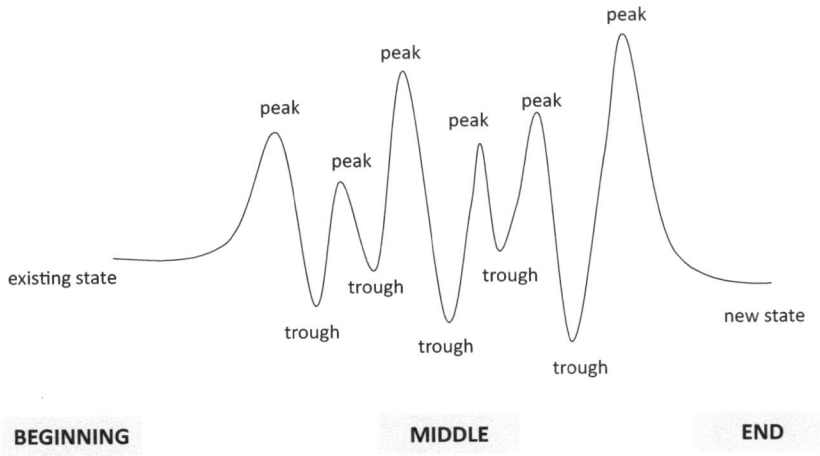

Fig. 7.2   The Story Wave

how and where they want to cut their case study—whether they would like to highlight just a specific set of peaks and troughs starting from a specific point of time or describe the entire situation from beginning to end, with a number of highs and lows.

Although not every case study is a dramatic event with numerous ups and downs, the story wave structure is suitable for case studies that trace the development, transformation and growth of organisations, institutions and nations because these occur over a longer period of time where there are shifts in environment and context. Here is an example of a strategy case where the organisation, SingTel Yellow Pages, faced a business crisis as the deregulation of the telecommunications market threatened the extinction of its business. SingTel Yellow Pages had to evaluate its strengths, weaknesses, opportunities and threats to determine its strategy options to remain relevant in a liberalised market.

Strategy Case Study

Charting a New Course

In 1997, the Singapore telecommunications industry was gradually being liberalised. SingTel Yellow Pages Pte Ltd (SingTel Yellow Pages), a subsidiary of SingTel, the only telecommunications service provider until then, would lose market share of the directory business. Racing against time to introduce a new business model and implement a new strategy and for a deregulated telecommunications market by 2000, SingTel Yellow Pages carefully considered its options.

From the beginning, SingTel Yellow Pages had focused on its cash cow, the Yellow Pages. It had made little effort to diversify because of its central belief 'if it ain't broken, don't fix it.' The product teams lacked field knowledge and was risk adverse. The company had depended on its relationship with the national Telco and did not have the ability to differentiate itself. The market was changing and information technology was knocking on its doors but the company was not ready to move.

There was a lot of external pressure on SingTel Yellow Pages to look at new technologies, new products and services, re-define its customer base and create new opportunities so that it could reduce costs, compete and survive as the market deregulates. SingTel Yellow Pages had to evaluate its core competence and resources, and consider a different approach to how it conducted its business.

Diversification might not be the only tool to address competition. It also had to be creative, be sensitive to user needs and leverage on technology.

Looking at the new environment ahead, it was likely that the successful directory publisher in any market could only succeed based on completeness. In a fragmented local telephone market, directory publishers could be an information arbitrage that owned comprehensive, wide-ranging, thorough information to better serve a sophisticated group of users. How should SingTel Yellow Pages transform itself?

SingTel Yellow Pages Pte Ltd

SingTel Yellow Pages had been the only telephone directory publisher since 1967. It was previously known as the General Telephone Directory Company (Singapore) Pte Ltd but was renamed Integrated Information Pte Ltd when the Telecommunications Authority of Singapore (Telecoms) fully acquired the company in 1985. In 1989, Telecoms was restructured and renamed Singapore Telecom (SingTel). The Telecommunications Authority of Singapore (TAS) was reconstituted and remained a statutory board with telecommunications regulatory functions. As part of SingTel's corporatisation programme, all Singtel subsidiaries were rebranded and Integrated Information Pte Ltd was renamed SingTel Yellow Pages Pte Ltd.

The SingTel Group, a telecommunication conglomerate, had extensive experience and linkages regionally and globally. SingTel Yellow Pages was able to tap on SingTel's networks and secured many publishing opportunities in the region. The identity of SingTel Yellow Pages was linked to that of the Yellow Pages. In other words, SingTel Yellow Pages and Yellow Pages were synonymous to both industry partners and the general public. Because of this, SingTel Yellow Pages had leveraged on the established Yellow Pages brand name.

As the official publisher of Singapore directories, SingTel Yellow Pages was able to develop a strong and comprehensive database of customers. Over the years, SingTel Yellow Pages had also established its infrastructure for printed directories and gained substantial experience and economies of scale in publishing and distributing its directory products. Unlike most directory companies in the world which purchased directory compilation systems from vendors or outsource the process to service bureaus, SingTel Yellow Pages had developed its own directory compilation system. This gave SingTel Yellow Pages the flexibility and speed of changing from one publication to another, enabled the development of multi-language products in English, Chinese and Malay, and supported product customisation.

SingTel Yellow Pages had 350 employees and distributed 3.5 million telephone directories in July annually. It maintained a 9 to 10 percent market share of the advertising pie, similar to other national directory companies in the USA and Europe. Like other telephone directory publishers in Asia, it inherited the database of the country's telephone subscribers by virtue that telecommunications had always started as a national project. It was in the mid-1990s that deregulation, liberalisation and privatising gradually usurped SingTel Yellow Pages's prime status. The Yellow Pages has been SingTel Yellow Pages's main source of revenue over the last 30 years. This problem became magnified with the liberalisation of the telecommunications industry. SingTel Yellow Pages had made many efforts to reduce dependency on the Yellow Pages by introducing niche directors and moving into neighbouring countries to explore publishing opportunities. It would take at least five to six years before the management could see a stable bottomline from these initiatives.

With the deregulation of the telecommunications industry in Singapore, three consortiums were bidding for Telco licence. These were Telecom One, StarHub and DirectLine. Each of these groups had the capability and experience to challenge SingTel and SingTel Yellow Pages in telecommunications services and directory publishing, respectively.

The Telephone Directory Publishing Industry in Asia

A common pattern in deregulation throughout Asia was the liberalisation of the telecommunication Industry. Regulatory bodies for telecommunication in Asian countries that were affected by this trend began to put out public tenders for various types of telecommunications services such as mobile communications, fixed-line communication, Internet access, value-added network, international communications and so on, to local and international companies. The conditions for the tender would be for several operators to compete for the same services or a combination of services within the same area or in different areas.

It was a standard requirement by telecommunication regulators, to expect the successful bidder of telecommunication licence to publish a telephone directory and provide telephone subscriber information for both users and the public. Regulators could stipulate that operator/s provided such information in one of all the following ways:

a. The traditional White Pages which carried listings of residential and business subscribers.
b. A business directory similar to the Yellow Pages which carried business listings of business subscribers classified in various headings that represented their trade or products and/or services that they offered.
c. An operator-assisted enquiry service to help the public locate the contact number of local subscribers.

The requirements of regulators varied from country to country. In more developed countries where information technology was dominant, for example, the European Union which had the EuroPages, subscriber information was available in both print and electronic form (compact discs, the Internet, Audiotex services). In less developed countries with lower adoption of information technology, traditional print medium dominated the scene.

These regulatory requirements were a challenge for the successful bidder to provide telecommunication services in the country. The core competence of the telecommunications company (Telco) was in telecommunications services and not publishing. To fulfil the requirements outlined by the regulator, the successful Telco would form a joint venture company with a commercial printer, print media owner or established directory publisher to produce the telephone directory. Another option for the Telco was to sub-contract the production to a publisher.

With the liberalisation of the telecommunication industry in Asia, there was opportunity for SingTel Yellow Pages to look into the surrounding markets, given its background, infrastructure, track record and regional networks. As Western markets were relatively more difficult to penetrate, many publishers look to developing nations, countries with non-existent or under-developed directory markets, as the next richest source of Yellow Pages growth opportunity.

Customers

The company's customers comprised advertisers and director users. SingTel Yellow Pages's advertisers comprised mainly small-and medium-sized businesses in Singapore. Advertisers chose SingTel Yellow Pages' directories because of its:

- regular publication,
- established advertising medium and a popular source of information for both local and foreign users,
- wide and guaranteed circulation with distribution to both residential and business subscribers,
- repeat usage by buyers when they look for information, and
- cost-effectiveness as compared to other forms of advertising on a per day and per unit basis.

In a customer satisfaction survey, advertisers claimed that they chose the Yellow Pages because it (in order of importance):

1. offered convenience in finding telephone number and addresses,
2. helped to attract new customers,
3. had market presence and a good company image,
4. contained a wide range of products and services, and
5. provided overseas exposure and trade enquiries.

In a separate market feedback report to the SingTel Yellow Pages management based on research conducted by the company's research unit, it was highlighted that advertisers were more discerning with their advertising budgets. They were willing to decrease their advertising programme with the Yellow Pages and migrate to other forms of advertising and promotions. They expressed concern about the need to get more response from their advertisement placement in order to justify the amount they have invested in the Yellow Pages. Advertisers were curious about SingTel Yellow Pages's plans regarding Internet commerce.

The other category of customers are the directory users. Over the last three decades, directory users had depended on and expected to obtain information of telephone subscribers from telephone directory or operator-assisted directory services. In a 1996 market tracking survey on Yellow Pages usage in Singapore, it was found that one in three buyers referred to the Yellow Pages when there is a need to buy and/ or to find out about a particular product/service, and when they were not sure of which company to contact. 93% of population were aware of the Yellow Pages. Although awareness was high, only slightly over half (56% of those who are aware of the Yellow Pages) used the Yellow Pages. The usage of Yellow Pages in 1996 (53%) was on a slight uptrend compared to 1995 (52%).

The Yellow Pages had some unique strengths inherent in the product. These included the wide-ranging information it carried, the ease of finding the required information, and the time saved in locating information. On the other hand, the survey results pointed out that buyers would check on an average of two information sources, probably one for background information and another to final decision. Yellow Pages provided a platform to gather data for analysis.

Deregulation brought about a different set of problems for SingTel Yellow Pages's telephone subscribers. Given that there were now multiple service providers, to contact a subscriber, you would need to know the carrier used by the subscriber before you could locate his contact details. This became a hassle for the general public. Previously, some subscribers would request for telephone numbers to be unlisted because of personal or business reasons. After deregulation, it was unclear how the new operator would handle this sort of situation. For those who subscribed to more than one carrier, users would be at an inconvenience since they would need to search through multiple directories to find the number that they were looking for. There could also be a situation where the number was not listed in any directory at all.

Businesses could require that the listing in the directory be formatted according to their existing operations. For strategic or historical reasons, businesses might use different carriers to meet their telecommunication needs. There could be problems integrating the fragmented information from different carriers into the directory. This surfaced the issue of deciding which directory to list and what to list so that users can find the information that was required.

Competition

The local competition is a threat to SingTel Yellow Pages because they could substantially reduce SingTel Yellow Pages's revenues and profits. Once the local competition offered products and services that were on par with those of SingTel Yellow Pages's or produced seemingly better alternatives (whether differentiated by lower prices, more benefits or other advantages), it was likely that advertisers and consumers would consider and switch to these alternatives. Choice, in itself, was a threat to SingTel Yellow Pages.

The existing competition in the current advertising industry included newspapers, radio, cinema, television, magazines, newspapers, buses, taxis and posters (see Table below on *Market Share and Revenue of Advertising Media in Singapore*).

Market Share and Revenue of Advertising Media in Singapore

Rank	Media	Market Share (%)	Revenue
1	Newspapers	46	S$580 million
2	Television	30.23	S$380 million
3	Yellow Pages	9.36	S$118 million
4	Magazines	5.45	S$68.4 million
5	Radio	5.18	S$65 million
6	Posters	1.73	S$21.6 million
7	Buses and Taxis	1.08	S$13.6 million
8	Posters	0.81	S$10.2 million

Trends in media spending showed that newspapers, television and the Yellow Pages were experiencing marginal growth in revenue as these media had established a good foothold and penetration in the market. Magazine revenue remained fragmented and stagnant as some titles dropped out of the rack only to be replaced with new titles (local and foreign). Radio appeared to be experiencing a second life. The success formula was focused on the needs of the listening public, such as members of Generation X, PMEBs (professionals, managers, executives and businessmen), uniform personnel, language, ethnic and dialect groups. Visual media such as posters, cinemas, buses and taxis were beginning to appeal to the members of public as the regulatory authorities relaxed rules on street advertising.

Substitutes

The Internet and Audiotex were substitutes to SingTel Yellow Pages's print directories. New developments in information technology, telecommunications and broadcasting have introduced new ways to connect buyers with sellers. Singapore's nation-wide high capacity network,

Singapore ONE, would deliver unlimited range of multimedia services to the workplace, home and school. Singapore ONE was operated by Singapore Cable Vision, Singapore Telecom and Singapore Communication Investments. This was a move to develop Singapore into an IT mega hub. Initially, the focus would be communications and media, electronic commerce and IT innovation. The authorities that regulate Singapore's communication industries had said that they would not stand in the way of companies entering each other's markets.

Suppliers

Each year, SingTel Yellow Pages would distribute 3,490,000 directories to the public. In 1997, telephone directories and the Yellow Pages used 7500 metric tons of news print (amounting to US$5 million). The challenge for SingTel Yellow Pages was to maintain sufficient stock of newsprint to meet printing requirements. It would forecast printing requirements and secure paper stock at an optimal price. However, the price of newsprint over the last five years had been erratic. In addition, SingTel Yellow Pages also had to consider storage costs, transportation costs, foreign exchange risks, efficiency of delivery schedule, options and insurance. Every year, SingTel Yellow Pages would invite key suppliers of newsprint suppliers from USA, Norway, Canada, China and New Zealand to tender for the project.

The magnitude of the order, type of paper, directory size, binding size, delivery schedule and printing process narrowed SingTel Yellow Pages's choice of printing companies to just one—Times Printers. SingTel Yellow Pages had awarded the contract of directory printing to Times Printers since 1983. Negotiation of this exclusive printing contract was done every five years. SingTel Yellow Pages would have to complete the entire contract before the company could terminate the contract. On the other hand, Times Printers were not allowed to print directories that competed with the Yellow Pages.

Database

SingTel Yellow Pages maintained an integrated database carrying information of all telephone subscribers in Singapore. It had made extensive use of its directory database. This had been the source of SingTel Yellow Pages's success in the last three decades and it continued to devote substantial time and resources to exploit this option. The database was segmented by demographics, geography, business and trade. SingTel Yellow Pages also supplied mailing lists to businesses and developed a call centre to provide telemarketing and fulfilment services for its customers.

There were other areas which SingTel Yellow Pages had thought of exploring. One was to use the database as the backbone for electronic directory, operator-assisted enquiring services and Audiotex. Advertisements, in the electronic products, could also be sold on their own or bundled together with print advertisements, thereby giving the advertisers the opportunity to reach out to customers who sourced for products and services in print and electronic media.

Businesses depended on the telephone directory for information. The information was used for correspondences, telemarketing and direct mail or as sales leads. This was an important source of information for businesses because incorrect information affected operations. In recent years, several directories and direct marketing companies had appeared in the market with directories and lists that were as accurate as SingTel Yellow Pages's. During a study on directory listings, SingTel Yellow Pages found that these companies had scanned SingTel Yellow Pages's directory using an Optical Digital Scanner and used SingTel Yellow Pages's database as their own. This was discovered because competing directories had the same mistakes found in SingTel Yellow Pages's publications.

Strategic Options

Liberalisation presented SingTel Yellow Pages with a set of new challenges. Since the announcement of deregulation of the telecommunications industry, new entrants would have already crafted their plans. SingTel Yellow Pages needed to pre-empt the competition. While it might not have the resources to implement all options at the same time, SingTel Yellow Pages hoped to be systematic in prioritising its plan of action and stay focused on its mission—*to meet our customer needs by providing a broad range of advertising media, marketing and information related services, in print and electronic modes, in local and overseas market, with quality service and excellent business performance.*

SingTel Yellow Pages considered these possibilities:

    a. create effective barriers of entry
    b. develop innovative products and services

a. *Create Effective Barriers of Entry*

One of the barriers of entry was to differentiate and create competitive advantage. SingTel Yellow Pages wanted to differentiate through superior product benefit and perceived advantage, low-cost operations, legal advantage, superior contacts, superior knowledge, sale advantages and offensive strategies. Sustained low-cost operations and economies of scale could translate into revenue for the company or passed on as advantages to users and advertisers. These are explained:

Strategies	Description
Demonstrate superior product benefit	Continue to maintain and develop good quality directories. SingTel Yellow Pages produced comprehensive directories. The Yellow Pages had been a dependable product, allowing SingTel Yellow Pages to achieve market leadership in the industry.
Accentuate perceived advantage	Due to superior product benefit and the universal brand name of Yellow Pages, SingTel Yellow Pages had established for itself a branding that was synonymous with reliability and quality.
Pursue low-cost operations	SingTel Yellow Pages's 30-year experience enabled it to explore and exploit low-cost process methodologies. The company's learning curve had flattened substantially compared to when it first started out. Indirectly, because of the company's experience, the entry barriers were raised for challengers.
Exploit legal advantages	SingTel Yellow Pages had secured copyrights in advertisements. It was the exclusive owner of established trademarks such as the Yellow Pages in Singapore.
Maintain superior contacts	SingTel Yellow Pages's sales force had built a strong relationship with its customers. It also had an extensive network of contacts with local and regional businesses.
Develop superior knowledge	More could be done to increase the level of creativity, innovation and initiatives in re-packaging and developing fresh and exciting products. SingTel Yellow Pages already operated its own integrated directory management and publishing system.
Exploit scale advantages	Ride on economies of scale and to take advantage of SingTel Yellow Pages's comprehensive infrastructure, publishing system and distribution channel for subscribers, printing companies, database and sales operations.
Develop offensive strategies	Use innovative advertising and promotion strategies. Leverage on its team of experienced and motivated sales force.

Creation of sustainable competitive advantage could be done through support activities, the organisation's infrastructure, human resource management, technology development, procurement, inbound and outboard logistics, marketing and sales, and services. Other competitive advantages that SingTel Yellow Pages could tap on would be through its operations but it was harder to pinpoint the salient advantages. On the whole, SingTel Yellow Pages's company processes, subscriber database, customer network and legal system were obvious areas for creating competitive advantages. The company's processes were crucial because they defined the workflow within the company. If carefully designed and implemented, the right work processes could increase efficiency and decrease cost to create the most effect combination of manual labour versus machine labour.

The subscriber database was the foundation of SingTel Yellow Pages's product. SingTel Yellow Pages's ability to provide an accurate and comprehensive directory for the population was its success factor. The customer network was SingTel Yellow Pages's competitive advantage. The closer SingTel Yellow Pages was to its customers, the more competitive advantage SingTel Yellow Pages had over others in the industry.

SingTel Yellow Pages's legal function could protect the company's products and processes. Through patents, copyrights and indemnities, SingTel Yellow Pages could creatively protect its products, brands and trademarks. This would be an effective barrier of entry to dissuade its competitors from imitation.

b. *Develop Value-added Products and Services*

To maintain SingTel Yellow Pages's position as the market leader by enhancing existing, developing and introducing new products and/or services.

Product Enhancements

Business Pages	Add business procedures; important telephone numbers; travel advisory and information (customs, immigration, transport, etc.); Chamber of Commerce and trade representative offices; convention and exhibition information and calendar.

Community Pages	Add calendar of events; emergency and non-emergency lines, hotlines and helplines; police stations and civil defence; sports, leisure and entertainment facilities; postal codes of buildings; transport (different modes, time schedule, routes, fare structure, etc.); maps (central business districts, shopping belts, island map); first aid and safety procedures for households; Audiotex information (consumer and information tips); Internet directory of business and informational websites.
Government Pages	Add directory of public services; directory of government and quasi-government departments.

New Products

Electronic Directories	Take advantage of the technologies available to cultivate new customers, advertisers, sales and production needs. Many directory publishers had introduced Electronic White and Yellow Pages to complement the printed version. Information in electronic directories was dynamic and more accurate as changes in listing were immediately transferred from the integrated database to the directory. New product lines and information could be easily updated.
Audiotex Services	Offer 1-800 and 1-900 services through talking advertisements (user would be directed to pre-recorded commercials), fax-on-demand, and Call-Connect.
Operator-assisted Yellow Pages	Offer users brand name information, opening hours of advertisers, location, acceptance of credit cards, schedule of events, geographical directions, etc. For example, a caller looking for flower delivery service on Mother's Day would be directed to a florist near his/her home which accepted credit card payment and provided weekend delivery service. This would benefit people who were on the move (e.g. mobile phone users), who needed instant information but had no access to a directory. A Call-Connect service could be incorporated to link the user directly to the company (e.g. the florist) which he/she was looking for.

Besides these two options, SingTel Yellow Pages wanted to lobby TAS to support SingTel Yellow Pages's initiative to maintain the integrated database and retain its role as an official telephone directory after the market liberalised. To do this, SingTel

Yellow Pages had to show distinct value-add and demonstrate operational excellence.

Rethinking Strategy and Business Model

SingTel Yellow Pages faced the challenge of choosing the right strategy—one that would likely fill the gap, achieve its goals and allowed flexibility for adaptations. The new millennium was one and a half years away. SingTel Yellow Pages was already behind time in positioning its business. It had to re-assess the company's core competence, identify new products and markets, and affirm its value chain. How should SingTel Yellow Pages develop a sustainable strategy and business model for a deregulated market?

Source: Adapted from Dennis Tan (1998) 'Developing A Strategy for a Telephone Directory Publisher Facing Deregulation. A Study of a Singapore Telephone Directory Publisher'.

Sometimes, events are more complicated, especially if you are writing a knowledge-capture case study to trace the transformation of organisations or projects over a long period of time. When this happens, there are opportunities for you to develop supporting stories, such as box stories or as exhibits in the appendix, or write another independent case study.

A Pinnate Venation storytelling form has a core story as well as several sub-stories. This type of story form is called the Pinnate Venation after the vein formation of leaves (Fig. 7.3). The main narrative branch has its own beginning, middle and end while the subsidiary or supporting stories have their own beginning, middle and end.

Using the Pinnate Venetian story form, the *Charting a New Course* case study could be told with a primary case and several secondary cases where the primary and secondary cases could be used together or independently (Table 7.1). Each secondary case study could have its own beginning, middle and end.

With finite time and resources, you must be precise about the cut of your story, that is, where and when you want to start and end your story, and how many subordinate stories or plots (if any at all) you want to include. As with all case studies, be clear about the purpose, target reader and context of your case study.

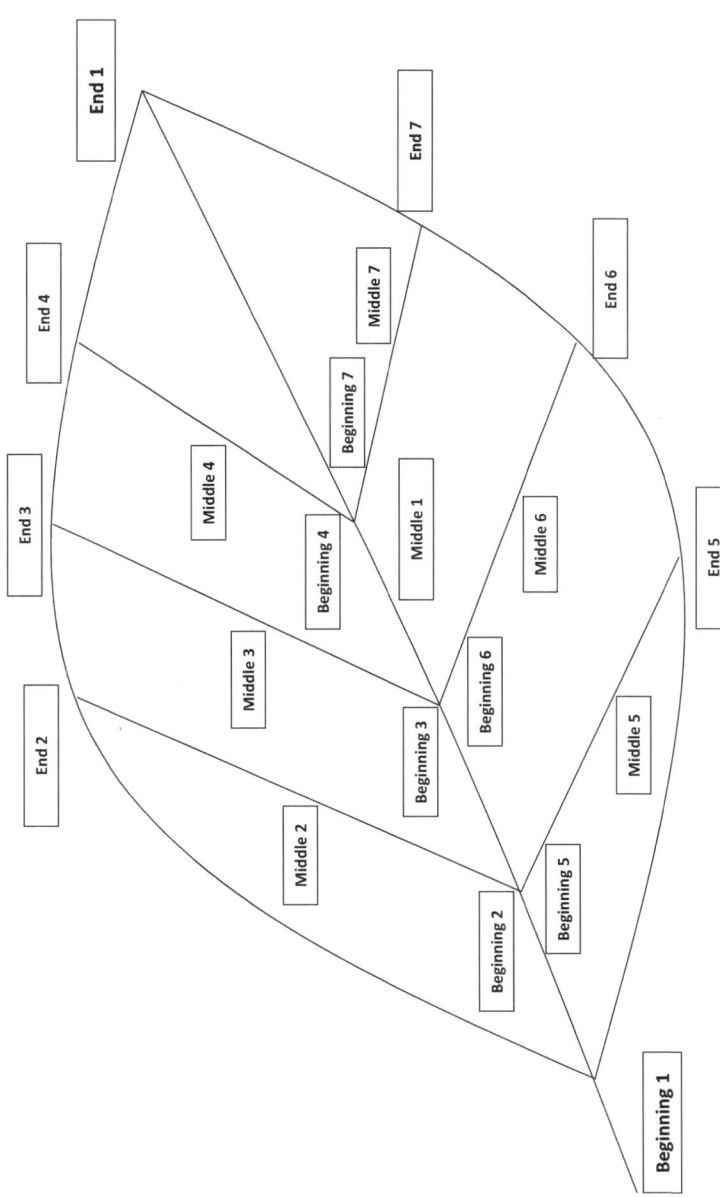

Fig. 7.3   The Pinnate Venetian

Table 7.1   Primary and secondary case studies

Primary Case		
Business Strategy for SingTel Yellow Pages in a Liberalised Telecommunications Industry		
Secondary Case 1	**Secondary Case 2**	**Secondary Case 3**
SingTel Yellow Pages product and market diversification strategies	Innovation strategies leveraging on new technologies and new product development	Deregulation of the Singapore telecommunications industry cluster

7.4   THE COMPARATIVE CASE STUDY

The goal of writing comparative case studies is to identify similarities and differences between two entities, analyse them, interpret the findings and convey new ideas about specific topics. During my research on the use of design management practices in organisations, I had compared how two public transport organisations—the Régie Autonome des Transports Parisiens (RATP) Group and the Land Transport Authority (LTA)—implemented design strategies in the development of their rail systems. In this study, I wrote separate case studies on the RATP and the LTA, using common parameters such as size of rail network, mission and vision, design management expertise, organisation history, attitudes towards art and design, and national culture, as section headers for the case studies. These common parameters helped to organise my thinking and gave me common units for comparison.

Here is my example of a comparative case study to help you model or adapt your own comparative cases. You will notice that it follows the Case Jigsaw of Beginning, Middle and End where context setting of each city follows the Introduction. In the Middle, the details of each organisation and how they use art and design are explained. The conclusion wraps up the case study comparisons with a conceptual framework. The style of writing is mainly expository because the purpose of this research case was to explain the 'how', 'what' and 'why' of the crisis for analysis and commentary. The final section titled Conclusion proposed a framework. This case study has a stronger author voice because its goal is to persuade readers to accept the author's analysis and recommendation as a result of the case comparisons.

Comparative Case Study

Culture as Strategy

1. *Introduction*

Art and design are an organisation's strategic resource and competitive advantage. The idea emerged because of the increasing fragmentation of markets and societies, and the irrationality of people and events. People and organisations are looking for a different purpose to life and to return to the fundamentals of living. They are looking for a new ritual, one not based solely on economics but on consistency and on meaningful interactions with others while living out their role in life. Because art and design are always dealing with intangible results that involve moral sentiments, emotions (happiness, anger, sadness, etc.) and sensory responses (shape, colour, balance, style, etc.), they can bridge the gap between hard disciplines like engineering, manufacturing and information technology, and human needs.

Art and design as strategic management tools is about how organisations incorporate these elements into their management strategies, processes and structures to create meaningful goods, services and experiences to change human behaviour, communities, industries and cities. It empowers the organisation to return meaning to the lives of people and transform humanity. The case studies on the Régie Autonome des Transports Parisiens (RATP) Group and the Land Transport Authority compare and contrast the use of art and design in two very different organisations.

For organisations that offer public goods and services, it is difficult to separate the organisation's strategy from the city's heritage. Two distinct cities, two different organisations. Paris birthed an organisation best placed to pursue a cultural strategy while Singapore founded one that excelled in competitive strategy. The centre of any city is often perceived as its financial or shopping district. The real centre of a city is its rapid transit system, simply because it is about enabling people to perform their different roles in life, satisfying their diverse needs and fulfilling the need for mobility. The organisations that develop and manage the rapid transit systems wield great power in moving people from one place to another while, at the same time, allowing them to embrace the spirit of the city, helping them to re-affirm their heritage as well as reinforcing a sense of meaning.

2. *A Case Study of the Régie Autonome des Transports Parisiens (RATP) Group*

2.1 Art and Design in Paris

The history, people, geography, religion and language of France had resulted in a distinct national identity that permeated all aspects of the country, including French organisations. French art was unique in its capacity to filter and assimilate. It was this same attitude and spirit that made Paris immensely successful as the country's centre for the arts. Paris is filled with historical relics and heritage of the city's art history, many of which retained their original structure and form even today. The Louvre, Palais Royale, Notre Dame, Montmartre, and many more, are part of the Parisian landscape and Parisian life. Each of them has a story; a history which was embedded in the heritage of the city and its people. These are a part of the day-to-day lives of Parisians. Heritage and culture are the value propositions of Paris and the challenge was for Parisians to be constantly reminded of the joy of living a simple life not motivated by consumerism.

Traditionally, the French concepts of art and design embraced a strong element of décor and style, easily seen in the elaborate architecture of Sacré Coeur, Notre Dame and Palais Royal. Artistic expressions were revealed through architecture, sculptures, paintings, landscapes, fashion, furniture, furnishings and more. The concept of products, or objects, can be a complex and philosophical issue. They are complex entities that provide both form and function. Both of these aspects of art and design are important in creating meaning for people.

2.2 The Paris Métro

It is within this philosophical backdrop that the Paris métro was born. The Paris métro is the second oldest métro in the world (1900), after the London Underground (1864).[2] Although discussions and planning for the métro started as early as 1871, the decision to finally proceed with the construction was eventually spurred by The Universal Exposition which was to be held in Paris in 1900. This also prompted the planning of other iconic projects such as the Eiffel Tower (1889). The State was forced to commit to building an underground rail system that could move the high volume of visitors expected to visit the exhibition.

The State and the Ile-de-France region financed the métro and the tramways. The Syndicat des Transports d'Ile-de-France (STIF), formerly the Syndicat des Transports Parisiens (STP), was the transport authority that manages public transportation in the Ile-de-France region. When the STIF was first set up in 1959, it comprised representatives of the State and eight Ile-de-France departments which were under the governance of the Préfet de Paris (Paris prefect). The board of directors of STIF had 34 members that represented the French State and local authorities of Ile-de-France.

There were a total of 22 regions in France. The Ile-de-France region was both a state territorial district as well as a local and regional authority. With an area of 12,000 square kilometres, it had 11 million residents and 60 million visitors per year. The Ile-de-France had 211 km of metro, 14 lines and 380 stations. RER[3] (Réseau Express Régional) or Regional Rail Network lines were jointly operated by the RATP and Société Nationale des Chemins de Fer Français (SNCF).[4] Public transport was regarded as a fundamental element to promote social and economic well-being.[5]

In 2003, the Paris métro had 3555 trains serving more than 4.35 million passengers every day, or 1190 million passengers every year (or estimated 4,467,000 people per day).[6] There were altogether 14 metro lines that covered 211.3 km. These 14 lines service 297 stations. The average speed of a train was 25 km/h, or about 100 seconds from one station to the next.[7] Métro lines were colour-coded and there were large signage systems to guide commuters. Network plans were also found in every station and maps were freely available at the counters. Single tickets cost Euro$1.30 while a *carnet* (book) of 10 tickets cost Euro$9.60. There were various ticket packages to cater for single day travel, monthly passes, weekly passes, or passes for visitors to Paris.

2.3 Art and Design Management in the RATP

The Régie Autonome des Transports Parisiens (Paris Metropolitan Transit Authority) or RATP in short, was set up in 1948 as a public utility company with financial autonomy. It provided up to 75% of overall passenger traffic for public transport. The RATP was a national company supervised by the government with the responsibility to operate all metro and bus lines formerly owned by the Compagnie du Métropolitain de Paris or CMP (Paris Metropolitan Railway Company) and the Office Regional des Transport Parisiens or ORTP (Public Transport Company of the Paris Region) respectively. The RATP managed the Paris métro, Lines A & B of the RER (Regional Express Network) train system that ply the Greater Paris Area, the Paris bus network and the Paris tramway system. Almost 10 million trips were made on RATP services every day in 2003.

The RATP Group had seven subsidiaries and 21 sub-branches with business areas that span transport, property, technology and trade. The Group's goal was to be involved in all areas of urban development within the Ile-de-France region, the provinces or abroad.[8] The 2000–2006 State/Region Plan Agreement identified that the priority would be in the provision of public transport. This constituted 40% of all projects undertaken and 3.07 billion Euros.[9]

Headquartered at Gare de Lyon, the RATP employed around 40,000 people in 2003. The RATP board comprised 27 members including government representatives, representatives from RATP employees, representatives from local elected officials, passenger representatives and a transport specialist. The chairperson of the RATP was appointed by Prime Ministerial decree upon recommendation from the Minister of Transport. Funding for transportation in Ile-de-France came from a combination of these sources: the Regions, the State and transport operators themselves, like the RATP.

The RATP's mission comprised these three components: to provide a network and space for social cohesion, to provide access to work and other activities, and to partner the physical mobility of the residents. Here, physical mobility referred to both physical and mental journeys. RATP was concerned about the well-being of the commuters in terms of physical and mental well-being when they travel. The RATP positioned itself as a partner to everybody's life in Paris (*un bout de chemin ensemble* or "on the way together").

The métro's first line from Porte Vincennes to Porte Maillot became operational on 19 July 1900. It was developed during a period of time where Paris had been rejuvenated and transformed under the influence of Baron Haussmann. The engineer, Fulgence Bienvenüe was responsible for construction works while architect Hector Guimard was in-charge of the Art Nouveau entrances. Guimard was a neo-classic art architect commissioned by the chairman of Compagnie du Métropolitain de Paris (Paris Metropolitan Railway Company) at that time to design station entrances. The Guimard entrance initiative was a conscious attempt to use art and design to achieve specific purposes: create visual markers for métro entrances, complement the urban landscape and the heritage of Paris, and express the aesthetic trends/movements of the culture during that period.

Guimard was given the brief that station entrances should be the stimuli of urban utopia, be environmentally friendly, complement street communication, and incorporate the nouveau style. This was the beginning of the use of art and design to meet a combination of objectives—the entrance was functional (it helped commuters locate the entrance to the underground station), meaningful (expressed the values and attitudes of the city's leadership and visions) and a culturally symbolic (represented art nouveau movement of the period) icon of the urban heritage at that time. Among the first and still remaining entrances of plant and floral motifs is Abbesses station on line 12 which was completed in 1900. This entrance is still a powerful visual legacy of the Paris heritage.

The purpose of art in the métro was not art for art's sake. It fitted into the doctrine of the métro, integrating with the métro space, and rationalised the use of space while conforming to certain pre-set design guidelines. Indirectly, art was also good for the organisation's image especially when the RATP operated in a city rich in heritage. Art helped to bring culture and instill sensibilities into everyday life. Art was a means for the RATP and the city's policymakers to connect with its residents and enhance the city-resident relationship. For example, incorporating poetry on publicity posters onboard trains expressed the culture of a people and their lives in the city.

Art was most visible in station architecture. Although the RATP owned art collections and there were instances where art had been incorporated into interior design initiatives, these were less visible.

In fact, the interior architecture of the organisation was considered a design output, similar to corporate stationery, signage, branding and other products. Art and design initiatives such as the re-introduction of design to three major developments which were the development of métro entrances, the launch of the Météor line, and the Centenary stations helped to create the métro's current reputation and increased the visibility of design.

After more than a century, Guimard's entrances remained endearing symbols of the Paris métro even when they had lost their effectiveness because the urban landscape of Paris had changed dramatically since the 1900s. In 1998, line 14 or Météor line featured a driverless train with silent rubber tyres to reduce noise and vibration. Other innovations included the set-up of a new multimodal transport hub at La Defense, an area west of Paris, to further integrate transport into the lives of Parisians. The La Defense and Gare de Lyon transport hubs made deliberate attempts to incorporate spatial design and information service design to improve navigation for commuters and improve their demand for other forms of transport such as trams, buses and high-speed trains.

The cultural dimension of the RATP originated more than a century ago where métro managers at that time started to include art in the stations. This practice endured and the RATP continued to receive sponsorship proposals from organisations to incorporate culture into the stations. The purpose of cultural programmes was to entertain commuters and improve their physical and mental wellbeing, including relieving their stress and boredom of travel. The cultural strategy was part of the design policy so that there was coherence of an overall vision to harmonise design through the transport network and raise the cultural value of the métro rather than randomly incorporating artworks into the architecture and the existing environment. In the same manner, art supported design by decorating the station entrances such as those for the Centenary celebrations. To celebrate the Centenary year of the Paris métro in 2000, the RATP collaborated with artists and architects to renovate or re-create some of its more significant stations.

The RATP believed that every physical journey (the movement from one place to another) had a corresponding mental journey (commuter moods, their role in life, the rhythm of the city) that was different for every person. Hence, the organisation sought to understand, provide for and define actual human needs, and not what commuters perceived they need. Cultural programmes included the development and management of permanent and temporary cultural facilities, and also the planning and organisation of regular events in métro and railway stations.

The RATP's Cultural Action had been guided by these principles:

- **Enhance the French Heritage**: The Paris métro is both a heritage and a cultural asset and the RATP is its mouthpiece. Through the cultural branding of the métro environment, the RATP hoped to gradually build up the less visible cultural values of the city. These values were promoted through the preservation and enhancement of artistic, architectural or industrial works throughout the métro network such as the Austerlitz viaduct and the Guimard métro entrances. Souvenirs representing old and contemporary heritage were created and sold as merchandise. The RATP also involved itself in programmes such as Heritage Days to develop industrial tourism activities.

- **Promote Events**: The RATP used events to create the experience of travel and integrate the métro into daily life. It leveraged on events that were linked to current festivities in the city to provide a diversion from routine day-to-day travel. The RATP also supported regular events such as the Spring of Poets or billboard campaigns which invited commuters to participate in different aspects of urban living.

- **Create the Environment**: Many métro stations were thematically designed to appeal to the commuter's senses (Centenary stations). Station design décor were designed and built in such a manner that they could be renewed and changed over time.

- **Create Cultural Installations**: Related to the above point on the environment, cultural installations referred to the station installations (exhibits and sound and image displays). These functioned as temporary exhibits. They entertain commuters during travel.

- **Commission and Install Public Art Works**: Public art works were considered as interactions between the artist and the public. Public art helped to "enhance transport in the imagination of the public"[10]. They also functioned as urban landmarks. Some of these public art works included Place Colette métro entrance by Jean-Michel Othoniel and the Siptrott's Les Gardiens on the outdoor concourse at La Défense.

Design in rapid transit supported the function of transport by making it more efficient and creating new value for travel. However, because of the integrative and holistic nature of design, it was less visible as a separate and independent entity. The shortcoming of this was that it had been harder for the public to see its value and appreciate its worth, unlike art, which was highly visible and decorative. In the physical environment, design was important in creating geographic identity through the visual treatments. The design of human space was crucial because it created positive travelling experiences which at the same time down-played the negative moments.

Environmental comfort such as temperature, acoustics, smell, touch, cleanliness, accessibility, reduction of vibrations, and even passenger safety could create the necessary sensitivities needed for a positive métro experience. RATP's design strategy had a socio-cultural role of transporting Parisians and also helping them to continually re-discover the city's unique heritage and culture.

Design in the RATP originally emphasised component design (vehicles, furniture, street furniture, rolling stocks, etc.), environment design (stations, sound environment, shops and commercial spaces, etc.), graphics (visual identity, signage, etc.), staff uniforms and the Web.[11] More recently, design also emphasised enhancing the commuters' experience during their journey. The multi-modal transport hub at La Défence station was an example of a borderless transport experience. RATP also adopted new technology and mechanics to invent new ways of moving people, and set new standards for the industry. In fact, the culture-centric organisation's most valued asset was its ability to change behaviours.

3. *A Case Study of the Land Transport Authority*

3.1 Art and Design in Singapore

The art and design ideology in Singapore was markedly different in spirit and outlook because of the city's age, history and its stage of development. Like Paris, the development of Singapore art and design initiatives was directly linked to the country's history, policies and economics. In 1959, Singapore broke away from Malaya and attained self-government. This posed huge challenges for the island's leadership in terms of public governance. There were insufficient jobs, the city lacked natural resources and skilled labor. The mandate of the leadership during that time was to create employment through investments. Achievement of economic goals was the key consideration for the city and the government had to ensure that the population remained employed. Manufacturing and other industrialisation efforts helped to create jobs for Singaporeans. Disciplines such as engineering, technology and science that can contribute towards commerce were the focus, not art and design.

Although the city's Ministry of Culture was set up during this time, its progress and impact on Singapore art was minimal. Art in the community was overshadowed by the need for employment, survival, racial cohesion and nation building. By the end of the 1960s, the focus on art education had declined. To keep up with global developments, Singapore's education system stressed the importance of science over art.

More formalised efforts for the arts came later when the Festival of the Arts was inaugurated in 1978. In the 1980s, there was a resurgence of government attention on creativity as an engine for future economic growth. During this period, high-tech, knowledge and services industries became the new core of Singapore's economic activity. It was also during this time that an economic committee was set up to look at new opportunities to further Singapore's competitiveness. The committee recommended that all aspects of economic activity be promoted. Art and design began to grow in stature in terms of their perceived ability to benefit the economy.

In 1989, a report of the Advisory Council on Culture and the Arts led to the formation of the National Arts Council. Art and design became part of the lifestyle industry cluster and had the potential to bring new economic advantages to Singapore. This also coincided with then Singapore Trade Development Board's design initiatives. The Singapore design award was first launched in 1988 and the Singapore Design Council was set up in 1992 to promote the use of design as a tool for Singapore's trade promotion. The International Design Forum was a biennial event that featured the Singapore Design Award winners and Young Designer Award competitions. These were all initiatives to help manufacturers and companies achieve competitiveness through product differentiation.

The 2000 Renaissance City Report provided a blueprint to develop Singapore into a global arts city and to provide the cultural framework in Singapore's nation-building efforts. It mentioned that culture and the arts were important to Singapore because they enhanced Singapore's quality of life, sense of identity and attractiveness of the country. Singapore's premise of design, like its art and culture, was derived from an economic point of view. In 2002, the Creative Industries Development Strategy paper outlined the importance of the art and design to the development of Singapore's creative industries. The city's cultural vision remained deeply rooted in economic spirit.

3.2 The Mass Rapid Transit (MRT)

In comparison to the Paris métro, the history of mass transit as public transportation was relatively recent for Singapore. The idea of an efficient and reliable transport system for Singapore was first mooted in the 1960s. During that period, public transport was mainly provided by the government-owned Singapore Traction Company and 11 private companies. The 1960s was also a time when Singapore was experiencing the aftermath of British troop withdrawal from the country. Against the backdrop of the need for industry and nation building, a State and City Planning study was commissioned in 1967. The study indicated that a rail transit system was needed by 1992. More feasibility studies were carried out between 1972 and 1980, including the involvement of an independent team from Harvard University to confirm and reinforce the need for such a system. Finally, in 1982, construction work on rail transit began. This was the beginning of the rapid transit system, which is also known as the Mass Rapid Transit, or MRT.

In October 1983, a statutory board known as the Mass Rapid Transit Corporation was set up to steer the MRT development. In 1987, the Mass Rapid Transit Corporation leased the commercial operations of the MRT to a new company called the Singapore MRT Limited (SMRT). All stages and sections of the 67km long North-South and

East-West lines were completed in 1990. In 1999, SBS Transit Limited (previously Singapore Bus Services or SBS) became successful in its bid for the North East line. The Singapore Bus Company or SBS was a government-owned bus company that was set up in 1973 to improve the fragmented bus system and amalgamate all bus services.[12] This made SBS Transit Limited the second MRT operator in Singapore.

All companies that operate transport services were governed by the Public Transport Council (PTC), a statutory board whose role was to protect commuter interests in matters related to public transport routes and fares. It followed pre-specified standards on areas such as route planning and design, service efficiency, hours of operation, affordability and service information. The PTC would review these standards regularly with the Land Transport Authority (LTA) and public transport operators to ensure that commuter expectations were met.

The population of Singapore was 4.1 million in 2003 and had a population density of 6057 per sq km for the country's total land area of 685.4 sq km. The first MRT line in Singapore became operational in 1988. The MRT served approximately 200,000 trips a day. At the end of 2003, there were three main MRT lines and two Light Rail Transit (LRT) lines. These were the East-West line, North-South line, North-East line, Bukit Panjang LRT line, and Sengkang LRT line. Within the next 10 to 15 years, the LTA intended to expand the 128 km of MRT network to 240 km. The North East line opened on 20 June 2003. Fully underground and costing S$4.6 billion, it stretched 20 km in length and linked residents in the northern part of Singapore (Punggol) to the city within 30 minutes. It had 16 stations and 1 depot. Of these 16 stations, 13 had been equipped to function as civil defence shelters. At its launch, the North East Line became Asia's first fully automated underground heavy rail system where the trains on this line were driverless. This line also became the second major rapid transit system rail line to be built since the completion of the East-West and North-South lines in 1990 which were a combination of above- and below-ground rail systems.

The aspiration of the city was to have a world-class transport system. A good transport system was a compelling proposition for organisations to set up operations in the city and boost the city's human capital by attracting people to work and live there.

3.3 Art and Design Management in the LTA

The Land Transport Authority (LTA) was a statutory board formed under the Ministry of Transport on September 1, 1995, to lead and develop all land transport requirements of Singapore. Its mission was to provide a quality, integrated and efficient land transport system for the needs and expectations of Singaporeans, supporting economic and environmental goals. Economic goals referred to the goals of the city in developing a vibrant and progressive economy. Environmental goals referred to land transport policies that support a higher quality of life in general, especially with regards to reduced congestion, pollution, road accidents, and to ensure that there is good air quality. Value for money addressed the need to make public transport affordable to the masses as well as effective construction cost. The parameters that defined such a system were convenience, reliability, ease of use, comfort, affordability and competitive travel times.

The organisation had 3710 employees in 2002/2003. The LTA did not operate or manage the network. These were managed by separate organisations such as the Singapore Mass Rapid Transit Corporation, SBS Transit, Trans-Island Bus Services and so on. Management of MRT operations were outsourced to rapid transit operators such as SMRT Corporation and SBS Transit who bidded for the operations of respective lines through a government tender system. These companies managed the day-to-day operations of the respective lines and were responsible for the commercialisation of the lines. The onus was on the transit operators to run their lines to generate revenue while maintaining the standards set by the LTA. Generally, operators earned revenue through transport fares and advertising. Transport fare was set by an independent public transportation council with representatives from transport-related agencies and community groups. In 2003, public transport ridership (both rail and bus) was 4.2 million.

The LTA had been successful in developing a handful of stations which were handpicked to showcase iconic architecture that enhanced the city's image of excellence, high quality and world-class. Design of the Changi station and Expo station were strategic in this sense. Located at the Changi International Airport, design of Changi station aimed to impress travellers. Expo station was located at the Singapore Expo, an international exhibition and exposition for trade and consumer industries, where architecture helped to brand the city. Skidmore Owens + Merrill, Inc. designed the Changi station and Norman Foster the Expo station. The architecture of these stations were significantly different from the rest of the stations on the East-West and North-South lines because both stations were primed to showcase Singapore's modernity and innovation. The Changi station subsequently won the 2003 Lumen award for its organic and integrated approach towards lighting within the overall design of the station.

For the North East Line, the LTA developed an art in transit programme, making it the first MRT line in Singapore to have art integrated into the architecture of the station, such as through wall and floor finishes. Before the North East line, there was no concerted effort to incorporate art with infrastructural design. Both the East-West and North-South lines emphasised functionality, utility and practicality. There were minimal embellishments and art was an add-on to decorate station atriums after the lines are finished. When the East-West line was first launched, modern art was used to create a special ambience and respect for the environment. Sculptures and wall art were placed at the Raffles Place and Somerset stations while hanging art works adorned the Dhoby Ghaut station. Art was not integrated into the design of the stations but added after station design was finalised. These artworks served as station decoration and were piecemeal.

Artwork for each of the North East line stations was created by local artists who depicted, through their works, the culture and heritage of the local community. The programme's objective was to present the historical and geographical significance of stations to express the soul and spirit of the city. Artists were invited to express an interest in creating works for the stations. Each station of the North East line told a story of the city, its way of life and the philosophies and beliefs of the people of the city. Each artist was assigned a station, with only a few overlaps of one or two artists to certain stations. When assigning a station to the artist, LTA considered the artist's style, strength of applying the style to the medium, the artist's background, and the size and profile (geographically, historically and socially) of the station. An art review panel comprising internal and external art practitioners, educators and industry experts was also set up to evaluate the art works. The overall cost of developing and producing art for the

North East line was estimated at S$6.7 million[13] (about 0.1% of the cost of the entire line, which was S$4.6 billion). Architects were appointed through LTA's tendering and procurement system for the design of each station. The development and implementation was supervised by the architecture department who coordinated with the artists, architects, system engineers, structural engineers and so on to achieve the functional requirements.

The trains on the North East line had improved from the 1990s trains on the East-West and North-South lines. More considerations were made in relation to commuter comfort and disability access. New seats were wider for improved back support (ergonomics) and there were more standing spaces and grabs bars compared to the older trains which had narrower seats and more seating space. The new trains also had designated spaces near the train doors to cater for wheelchair access.

For the stations, lifts and ramps were included in the overall design as a standard requirement, together with a tactile guidance system. Disability access was never a consideration in the previous system. A roll-back plan was being implemented to retrofit all older stations with disabled lift access.

Stations located in suburbs followed a different design brief from stations located near important landmarks. Stations in the suburbs are more functional and simple while those near landmarks were more visually outstanding. Station designs in the suburb complement the surrounding landscape of public housing development flats while downtown stations were usually connected to office buildings where access into the stations were found within the buildings.

Station design for Marina line was developed through an architectural design competition first, followed by calling for a tender for design-and-build. The appointed contractor worked with the competition winners to build the Museum and Boulevard stations along the line. In collaboration with the Singapore Institute of Architects, competition rules and criteria were developed to invite architects to provide design for the stations.

Decision-making in design was guided by expert panels that comprised professionals in the art and design practices and/or industries. The Architectural Design Review Committee comprised local architectural experts while the Art Review Committee comprised representatives of the art community in Singapore. The Architectural

Review Committee provided guidance for design and the Art Review Committee for the art in transit programme. The committees provided the standards for art and design. Ability to meet project deadlines within budget was one of the indicators of maintaining standards, along with other indicators such as efficiency, safety, value for money and reliability.

4. *Conclusion*

The strategic orientation and execution of art and design strategies in the RATP and LTA are distinctly different even though both organisations are developers of the public rail transport system. An art and design-centric organisation is one that constantly rethinks the purpose and connections of good and services to change the culture of a society or an industry. Art and design as strategic management tools are the expression of this ideology. They are not used for aesthetic purposes but as part of a holistic, systemic framework to define new perspectives and strategies to achieve this mission. Not all organisations start out as being culture-centric. They go through different stages of development. Younger organisations tend to focus more on meeting the functional needs of their customers. As they mature, their strategic focus shifts.

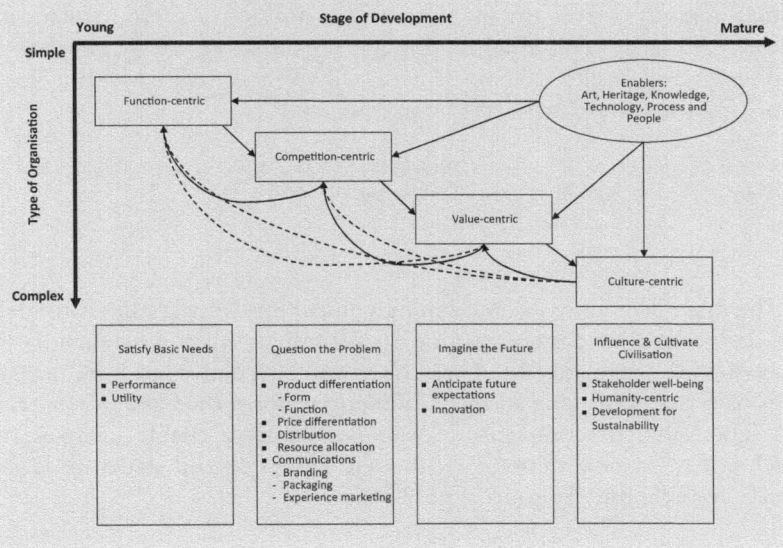

Fulfilling utilitarian needs as a primary function is augmented by reminding customers of their heritage and sense of self in the larger community. A seemingly ordinary physical good or service is transformed into a sensory, emotional and cognitive experience. The innovations are to form part of the community's heritage, shape the way the people think and understand their world, create new sensitivities and sensibilities in people and become part of the community's progress. This duality of the culture-centric organisation's vision creates a deeper purpose with a larger impact. Revenue generation and satisfying customer needs are by-products because the cultural strategy emphasises the invention of new goods and services for the cultivation of new behaviours which help to progress the community in terms of its social and economic developments. The inventions ultimately bring in value for the organisation and even advance the industry, although they were not the primary intents. These inventions also serve as new standards for the industry, allowing the organisation to create new possibilities, new values and new futures while preserving the heritage and culture of the community.

The culture-centric organisation is a philosophical, participatory and inventive entity; it critically questions the relevance of art and design in terms of their cultural value, social heritage, practical function, sensory impact and intellectual contribution. As intermediaries to create meaning and legacy for the organisation and its community, art and design have to be accepted and internalised within the organisation as part of strategic management.

Source: Adapted from June Gwee (2008), *Art and Design for Strategic Management: Culture as Strategy*, Saarbrücken: VDM Verlag Dr. Müller

The main take-away for developing comparative case studies is to identify key parameters for comparison so that they function as anchors for analysis. Next, compare the descriptions and alternatives to look for patterns to uncover insights and new thinking to form the basis of your theory. The value of comparative cases is that they enable analysis and development of new thinking or theory. This style and structure is also flexible for adapting for journal publication.

Process, strategy, crisis and comparative case studies can always be recasted as leadership case studies by adding a main character or protagonist into the case study and telling the events and incidents from the point of view of this main character. Having a protagonist in the case study can better connect your reader to the subject matter. But it may not be always easy to get individuals and organisations to be protagonists of your case study. Some decline because of sensitive issues mentioned in the case study, others refuse for personal reasons such as not wanting publicity.

7.5   THE MULTIMEDIA CASE STUDY

Case studies can be composed and delivered through a combination of words and moving images where text, graphics and animation are combined with music, voice-over and sound effects. These visual narratives can be found in games, simulations and eLearning courses. Visual narratives have become increasingly popular with a new generation of readers because the baby boomers, Generation X, millennials and Generation Z have grown up with film, television and the Internet. They are accustomed to receiving information and ideas through sight, sound and play.

There are two ways to produce multimedia case studies. The first method is to convert an existing text-based case study into a visual medium such as video or animation. The advantage of this method is that the concept of the story in the case study is already formed and framed. The challenge is to convert the content into a different medium which may require skills that the case writer does not have. In this instance, case writers will have to rely on another specialist (e.g. video producer, multimedia editor, copywriter, etc.) to repackage the text-based case study. During the conversion, case writers may find that they may need to collect additional data content, or drop existing content because it is impossible to translate word for word from text to visual. You can think of this as making a film based on the story in a novel. Sometimes, the original text-based case study may even limit the impact of the visual narrative if the case writer cannot imagine how the case study form can be converted to convey the story.

The second method is to directly conceptualise and develop a case study topic as a visual narrative without first writing a text-based version. Here, the case writer has to think in visual form—how to combine text, images and sound to tell the narrative of the case study so that it achieves its purpose. The advantage here is that a text-based format does not have to be created beforehand. Case writers directly develop the case study concept and design how 'readers' access and view the case study content. In addition to traditional skills such as research, concept development and writing, case writers also need skills in storyboarding, content design, scriptwriting or copywriting and digital storytelling.

The process of developing a visual narrative is the same as outlined in The Writer's Compass (Chap. 2). The main technical difference is in Steps 2, 4 and 6. In Step 2, the case concept plan must indicate which aspects of the visual narrative development is to be outsourced and the corresponding cost of outsourcing. Development of visual narratives can be costly depending on the specialist talents and equipment that are required. Stakeholder consultations are also more complex because there are more people involved, for example, programmers, producers, artists, technical directors, instructional designers and video editors.

In Step 4, write the case study in the form that is to be seen in visual format. The critical shift here is for the case writer to stop thinking of their target audience as readers and start thinking of them as viewers, learners and consumers of the experience.

If the case study is intended as a film or video, then write a script that contains columns for description of images, text, audio, timing and instructions on how to combine these (Table 7.2). Other details that are included are colour of the scene, angle of the shot, tempo of the music, feel of the composition (e.g. contemporary, antique, futuristic, present day).

If the case study is a visual narrative that is composed for digital learning, always consider the user experience and navigation on the digital platform. Case study content is organised according to the design of the user experience—how you would like the user to encounter the information, interact with it, relate to it and walk away with insights. The content is mapped to the user journey and vice versa. Case study content may have to be chunked and delivered in short bursts, but linked by a common visual or audio element across all units. The chunks of content can be little scenarios, vignettes of information or units of facts that can be sequenced.

After the content (whether in script, scenarios or vignettes) has been written and designed, develop a storyboard of the case study. A storyboard is a graphic plan of the narrative, shown by individual sketches or illustrations laid out in sequence. It organises and describes how the scenes of a story will unfold. Some storyboards have a short description

Table 7.2   A video script

Time	Visual	Audio
0:00:00	Fade in title: All Things Nonya: The Peranakan Shop	Fade in: background music—contemporary with faint and subtle Oriental instrumentation
0:00:10	EXT, DAY: Camera wide on Civic District building in foreground and city centre with busy streets in background. INT: Camera zooms into entrance of building and into entrance of the restaurant.	FX: street sounds and traffic sounds
0:00:20	INT: WS pan to female shopper walking towards shelf with Peranakan books. Dissolve to MS of female shopper browsing books.	Fade into VO. VO female shopper: I didn't expect to find a boutique bookshop in the business district. I work nearby and walk here for food and shopping. Now, I drop in every week to see if there are new items. VO female shopper: I like this bookstore because there are all sorts of things here related to Peranakan culture. It is cosy here and the people are helpful. I found out later that they were student volunteers.
0:02:28	Zoom out to WS of male shopper, retiree	VO male: Some afternoons, I come here with my wife. Usually, I read the books and she shops for clothes and knick knacks.
0:03:30	Cut to MS of shop owner with background of shop filled with items. SUPER: Lynn Lee, Manager WS pan of shop interior—shelves, coffee area, books racks, clothes, accessories, souvenirs. WS pan of shop space	VO manager: This is our smallest retail outlet—in terms of floor area, it is only 1000 sq m. On average, our outlets are around 1600 sq m. Although small, this boutique shop is a big milestone for us—it is the only shop in the business district that sells authentic Peranakan books.

below each thumbnail graphic to explain how the scene will be treated (Fig. 7.4).

The structure of visual narratives mirror that of text-based narratives because they are anchored in Campbell's monomyth and Freytag's pyramid. There is a beginning, middle and end with peaks and troughs within

Fig. 7.4 Storyboard of a video case study

a specific timeframe. Case-based games, simulations and scenarios, because they are written with real-world and fact-based narratives, are excellent for independent learning as well as team-based learning. Learners play out the event and are confronted with real decisions such as 'does the city have enough resources', 'how can an organisation improve productivity', 'how can communities innovate'?

Writing for games and simulations starts with creating the game world, characters and plot, which is similar to the narrative case structure. The key difference in writing for visual narratives is the emphasis on showing rather than telling. Visual cues are used to show context and create empathy. Images, sound, motion and text are combined in different proportions to depict a scene so that it captures the imagination of the viewer.

Some visual narratives are functional while others are aesthetic. Because visual narratives are experience-based, you have to first see the narrative as a whole comprising of different parts rather than the other way around. If you compose the different parts first, thinking that they can be eventually linked to form the whole, then the final narrative will risk being just a sum of individual small experiences joined together to support a theme. This is similar to how you have to use the Case Roundel to develop a case study concept plan first before using the Case Jigsaw to build individual components of your case study. The goal is to give the target audience a seamless story experience.

Next, the visual narratives are developed into prototypes and tested. This means that over a pre-determined timeframe, readers, users and learners can interact with the narrative. This allows the case writer and development team to collect information on the effectiveness of the visual narrative and use the information to refine and enhance the product before it is produced and launched.

7.6   THE STAR CASE STUDY

Many have attempted to find indicators to measure the quality and impact of case studies. Some of the common indicators are usage (how many times the case study has been purchased, downloaded, used in class or cited), reputation (who has cited or made reference to the case study and where has the case study been cited) and impact (the case study has brought forth new perspectives and contributed original thought to the field, inspired new areas of study, or caused key stakeholders to rethink the way things are done or change mindsets). While relevant, these indicators can only be captured in the medium or long term, they do not help a reviewer, editor or assessor of case studies decide whether a case study is good enough for publication or for use in the classroom.

Describing what makes a good case study and why a case study is good is as elusive as saying why you like a certain movie, book or a painting. There is a certain level of subjectivity which is specific to target audience (reader or learner) preferences. That said, I will still offer a list of broad criteria for you to use as a guide to determine the effectiveness of a case study. To make your evaluation and assessment more concrete, you may want to assign weights to each of the criteria to help you make a more objective decision.

Here are the basic features of a star case study.

a. Purposeful

It achieves the objective of why it is written, whether it is for discussion in class, to question assumptions, to record successes and failures, to re-think decisions and policies, or for research.

b. Real & Objective

It is based on a real issue that is relevant, complex and challenging. It describes a real issue or problem that has multiple options, possibilities, dilemmas and obstacles. The case study presents multiple sides of an issue to reveal the complexity of the problem and how it can be seen from different perspectives.

c. Contextual

It explains the context in which the issues/problems sit and where decisions had to be made. This is based on the premise that no decision is valid all the time nor in all circumstance and environments; problems evolve over time. Policies and strategies evolve over time and could be re-examined at regular intervals. Good case studies capture how policies and strategies changed as the environment changed.

d. Reveals Tacit Knowledge

It captures the rationales of decisions and actions, including the back and forth of discussions and the consequences linked to each decision.

e. Evidence-based

The case study is based on facts, whether secondary or primary data, even if disguised. Its content is a result of rigorous research and there are sufficient facts and information for in-depth discussion and analysis, without being excessive. The information presented in the case is neither too broad, too superficial nor too technical. Readers must be able to use the information to develop their own conclusions and derive new perspectives.

f. Significant

The case study contains issues that are important to individuals, businesses and countries or have direct or indirect impact on society. Because of their significance, it benefits readers to understand and identify with these issues.

g. Insightful

There are specific lessons to be learnt. It contains insights that appeal to the head (cognition and intellect) and the heart (human emotion and empathy). It compels readers to act by having passionate discussions about the topic, question their assumptions, or look for more information about what they have read.

h. Fresh

This is either a new story that has not been written about or the angle of the story is interesting and different from what has already been published. There is originality in the angle and perspective presented in the case study.

i. Current

The event might have concluded but the issues are still relevant and will be for at least two to three years. The lessons of success or failure remain applicable, and the skills, knowledge and attitudes that the case intended to raise are still topical.

j. Engaging

Readers are engaged and compelled to act after reading the case study. The form (the way the case study is composed and presented) and the function (the lessons found in the content) is correctly pitched to help readers achieve the purpose of the case study. If you can combine these tools to tap into readers' greater purpose, then it changes their perspective and motivates them to act or change their behaviour.

NOTES

1. MacEWAN, E. J. *Freitag'sTechnique of Drama: An Exposition of Dramatic Composition and Art by Gustav Freitag.* An authorized translation from the sixth German edition. Third Edition. Chicago: Scott, Foresman. https://archive.org/details/freytagstechniqu00freyuoft accessed on 18 April 2017.
2. White Paper, *A World Class Land Transport System,* (Singapore: Land Transport Authority, 1996), p. III.

3. This is a high-speed urban rail network in and around Paris. The RATP runs two of the four lines.
4. Syndicat des Trasports Parisiens. www.stif-idf.fr. Date last accessed: 22 Apr 2004.
5. London Assembly Transport Committee. *Transport in Paris: A Delegation's Visit to Paris.* July 2003, p. 9.
6. London Assembly Transport Committee, "Transport in Paris: A Delegation's Visit to Paris", July 2003.
7. RATP website. www.ratp.fr. Date last accessed: 21 Nov 2003.
8. RATP corporate website, http://ratp.fr/ratp_group/missions_goals/dvp_perspectives/538.shtml, date last accessed: 2 Sep 2004.
9. Ibid.
10. Ibid.
11. Yo Kaminagai, "Design at RATP, the Driving Force Behind Continuous Change". $N^0 20$ revue de design. (Azimuts: Nov 2001). p. 80.
12. Yong Phang Sock, "Singapore's Public Transport", (Singapore: National University of Singapore and Harvard University, 1999), p. 3.
13. "Line Drawing", *The Straits Times Life!*, (Singapore: Singapore Press Holdings, 2003).

CHAPTER 8

The Editor's Rubric

Tell the most complicated story in the simplest way.
Make every word count.

Editing is the process of reviewing and preparing content for publication or launch on the intended platform. During this process, the editor would correct, condense, modify, refine, remove mistakes and re-arrange text and/or images.

It is rare to achieve a perfect piece of written work on first try. Good writing, more often than not, is the result of many revisions which involves edits by the writers themselves, as well as by their peers and professional editors. Authors should always review and edit their own work. Writing is an individual activity and a creative activity. It is natural for writers to be so passionate about what they are writing that they develop blind spots related to content, language and structure. Therefore, it is always useful to ask someone else, preferably an editor who is also a content expert, to edit the work so that he or she can bring an objective and fresh perspective to the written work.

Similarly, for visual productions, a professional editor who is skilful in combining words, sound and images, as well as sequencing them, helps to improve the quality of a film or visual production. However, for the rest of this chapter, I will focus only on editing written text.

© The Author(s) 2018
J. Gwee, *The Case Writer's Toolkit*,
https://doi.org/10.1007/978-981-10-7173-7_8

8.1   EDITING THE CASE STUDY

The Editor's Rubric is a guide for case writers and editors to assess the quality of case studies. It also provides a benchmark for the expected quality (Table 8.1). To assess the quality of the case study, you can assign points for each category or sub-categories of the criteria.

Before editing begins, the editor should understand the purpose of the written work, its target audience and how it will be used in its final form. Always read the abstract or summary of the work, if there is one. More importantly, read the Opening to identify the angle or 'hook' of the case study. All relevant information should be provided for the reader to evaluate according to the 5 Ws and 1H (Who, What, Where, Where, Why, How). A good Opening foreshadows what to expect from the rest of the case study.

Editing a piece of work does not occur in a single sitting. Editors go over a piece of work many times. For written work, editors could read the draft at least four times in order to edit it thoroughly.

8.1.1   The First Reading

On the first reading, read the Opening of the case study carefully and focus on the structure. Structure refers to the arrangement of information, the categorisation of ideas, the flow of paragraphs and sentences, and logical ordering of information. Pay attention to the flow of ideas and how each segment has been categorised. The headings and sub-headings will signal whether the case study has been organised in the best logical order. Assess whether paragraphs frame ideas with logical transitions. The flow of thoughts should support the logic of the content. Check also if the headings are relevant to the sections.

8.1.2   The Second Reading

On the second reading, target content clarity and rigour. The issues should be clearly identified and support the angle of the case study. There should be clarity in terms of topic and issue. The description should also be in line with the actual. The quality and relevance of citations and quotations help the editor to assess the rigour of evidence in the content. Facts should be accurate and their description should form a coherent whole. Editors who are content experts value add by scrutinising the comprehensiveness of content coverage and assess whether there are repetitions or omissions. Check that facts are specific and definitive with no ambiguity. The content should

Table 8.1 Editing Rubric for case study

Criteria	Description	Strength	Weakness	Comments for author
Content • Clarity • Rigour	• Issues are clearly identified and relevant to the purpose of the case study • Sufficient level of detail, complexity and richness • Facts are presented clearly with no gaps or omissions, unless intended • Comprehensive coverage of information and discussion • Objective presentation of facts • Accuracy of facts • Coherence of content			
Structure • Arrangement of information • Ordering of ideas and issues	• Engaging Opening containing 5Ws and 1H • Paragraphs frame ideas • Best logical transition and flow of issues • Effective categorisation of ideas • Adequate inclusion of figures, charts, graphs, and so on			
Language and style • Quality of expression • Linguistic appropriateness	• Correct use of grammar and punctuation • Efficient use of words • Fluent and concise • Appropriate style and references • Correctly pitched to target reader			
Overall effectiveness	• Content and logic are aligned • Ease of reading • Engaging • Achieves purpose			

be comprehensive, relevant, objective and contain sufficient detail. Content and the logic of content should be aligned. Except for glaring errors, avoid polishing up the style and language during this first reading because if the content is lacking, then the entire case study may need to be re-written.

8.1.3   *The Third Reading*

On the third reading, take on the role of a proofreader to ensure that the words used are efficient and appropriate for the purpose of the case study and its target audience. This time, focus on the language itself—the grammar, style, efficiency of words, fluency, consistency and so on. Spell-check and grammar software can be the first line of defence to spot spelling and grammar mistakes. Be sure to comb through your work yourself or ask someone else to proofread the case study. Look out for spelling errors, grammar errors, repetitions, omissions and misused words. Ensure that the same form of spelling, punctuation, tenses and citations are consistently used.

Grammar, punctuation, fluency, consistency, conciseness and writing style should be appropriate to the issue presented. They should also be appropriate for the case study purpose. Check if the correct tenses and punctuation have been used. Ensure that words, phrases and ideas are clear, succinct, efficient and coherent. There should be efficiency in the choice of words used and simplicity in expression. Eliminate any redundancies and repetitions where possible, unless you are using for emphasis.

8.1.4   *The Fourth Reading*

Finally, on the fourth reading, look at the overall effectiveness of the narrative as a whole—the content, structure, language and purpose of the case study should be combined into an engaging and meaningful story. For example, a teaching case should be easy to read, interesting and engaging to the learner. The central issue should also be obvious and clear.

There are no rules on how many times or how fast an editor edits a piece of written work. It depends on the person's experience, knowledge of the subject matter and interest in the work itself.

8.2   Editing the Teaching Note

The same method can be used to edit a teaching note. The Editing Rubric for a teaching note is shown here (Table 8.2). The main difference between editing a case study and a teaching note is that the editor would need both subject area knowledge and basic knowledge of learning design.

Table 8.2 Editing Rubric for teaching note

Criteria	Description	Strength	Weakness	Comments for author
Depth and extent of analysis	• Analyses are relevant and achieve learning outcomes • Sufficient level of detail, complexity and richness in analysis • Facts needed for analysis can be found in the case study • Consequences of options are well described • Objective presentation of facts • Additional references and follow-up facts have been provided			
Teaching plan	• Learning outcomes are clearly described • Teaching approach achieves learning outcomes • Time plan is practical and achievable • Board plan is comprehensive and coherent			
Application of theory/model	• Correct application of theory/model • Case issues support theory and practice • Links to other theories are considered and provided			
Overall effectiveness	• Analysis, learning objectives and teaching method are aligned • Clear and reader-friendly • Useful for a first-time instructor			

PART VI

Teach

CHAPTER 9

The Case Method

Critical thinking can only be learnt, not taught.

The case method is a teaching approach where learning occurs through facilitated discussion led by a skilled instructor within a classroom environment. It is based on the idea of learning by doing. Learners are expected to identify the issues described in the case, evaluate the possible options, decide on an option, justify it and propose an action plan to implement the solution. Learners are forced to take on the roles and responsibilities of specific people in organisations, grapple with their dilemmas, formulate strategies, suggest recommendations and defend their choices. Through this process, learners develop sense-making skills, decision-making skills, critical thinking skills, communication skills, listening skills and self-reflection skills.

A teaching case is usually written in the narrative style because its goal is to place learners in the shoes of the decision-maker and immerse them in the events and actions of the story in the case so that they can experience real world challenges when developing decision-making skills. This is also a good structure for reading cases because it engages readers to learn on their own.

Well-written and properly-led cases force learners to search for multiple alternative solutions, weigh those solutions and finally recommend and

© The Author(s) 2018
J. Gwee, *The Case Writer's Toolkit*,
https://doi.org/10.1007/978-981-10-7173-7_9

defend one. They should also be able to identify critical success factors, identify constraints and opportunities, as well as detect critical omissions in the given situation. In a teaching case, solutions may not be directly described in the case study and it would be up to the learners to analyse, debate and develop their own recommendations.

Discussions in class should develop and test ideas so that collectively, learners have a richer and deeper understanding of the issues raised in the teaching case. However, the quality of the discussion depends on the extent of learners' preparation before class, their participation in class, and the facilitation skill of the instructor. The instructor can be the case author or a resource person who has knowledge of the content of the teaching case. More critically, the instructor should be an expert facilitator. If the instructor is not the case author, then the instructor may need more teaching aids and content support.

The design and composition of the teaching case is led by pedagogy which is informed by the instructor rather than the case writer. Hence, it is the job of the case writer to find out how the instructor is going to teach the case study. The case writer must keep handy the two 'W's— you must know why you are writing the case study and who you are writing for.

9.1   THREE-PART LEARNING APPROACH

The case method learning approach is divided into three parts: individual preparation by learners, small group discussions and large group discussions. The teaching case and a list of three to five discussion questions are given to learners at least two weeks prior to the case class. This gives learners sufficient time to read, prepare on their own and conduct small group discussions before the actual class.

During individual preparation, the learner reads the teaching case, analyses it, and develops the strategy or action plan from the point of view of the decision-maker described in the case. It is normal for learners to take up to two hours to prepare on their own.

After learners had a chance to think through and plan on their own, they should get together in a small group of five to eight persons to discuss their analyses and proposals. During the small group discussions, there may be revisions to the individual learner's analysis as more ideas surface and previous assumptions are challenged, forcing the group to think deeper and harder about the issues and problems outlined in the case.

Finally, learners attend the case class which is a large group discussion led by an instructor who facilitates the discussion process. At university level courses, large group discussions could comprise 60 to 80 learners. The case method is more effective when there is active learner participation and when the class is facilitated by an instructor who is an expert in the facilitator process and has good content knowledge of the teaching case that is being discussed. In universities, class participation in a case study discussion can form 50% of a student's grade, which greatly incentivises learners to contribute in class.

The instructor assesses the students on their ability to:

- Define the problem and issues
- Sense-make the environment in which the problem occurred
- Justify relevant and appropriate analysis of the situation
- Present clear, evidence-based and well-argued plan of action

9.2   DESIGN OF THE LARGE GROUP DISCUSSION

The case method supports the process curriculum model (Smith, 1996, 2000)[1] where learning occurs through the interaction of learners, knowledge and instructors where they discuss, analyse and debate to create meaning and make judgements about issues. The effectiveness of such a curriculum model is dependent on the skill of the instructor in facilitating the learners towards the learning outcomes, as well as involving and motivating learners to participate in the learning. Some of the considerations are:

- Decide on the first questions to open the discussion
- Determine how to reinforce the major issues and central themes in the teaching case
- Establish the critical issues and the connections between issues
- Identify the logical and analytical errors that learners may make and how to enable them to reflect and learn from these errors
- Decide where to focus attention and re-direct attention of learners
- Consider variations of the discussion (e.g. role play, games, simulations) and if these would be effective in achieving the learning outcome
- Develop a plan for recording discussion points on the white boards
- Decide on how to close and wrap up the session

The case method is a highly cognitive instructional method which can be incorporated as part of instructional design theories such as Gagné's Nine Events of Learning[2], Kolb's Experiential Learning Cycle[3] and the Honey and Mumford Learning Cycle[4] which is a variant of Kolb's Experiential Learning Cycle. I have chosen to illustrate how the Gagné and the Honey and Mumford models can be used in the design of case method sessions because I have used these in my case method sessions.

9.2.1   *Events of Learning*

Gagné's Nine Events of Learning describes nine sequential events necessary for effective learning. These nine events occur sequentially starting with gaining attention, informing learners of objectives, stimulating recall of prior learning, presenting content, providing learning guidance, providing feedback, assessing performance, and enhancing retention and transfer to job.[5] Gagné's model is based on the premise that basic concepts must first be understood before learners can move on to a higher level cognitive activity.

A teaching plan can be designed using Gagné's Nine Events of Learning, starting with events 1 to 3 where the learning contract and recall of prior learning are established (Table 9.1). Instructors proceed to introduce theories, models and concepts which are part of event 4, followed by clear instructions of how to learn the content. To practice and apply the concepts taught in event 4, the case method is used in event 6 to elicit actual performance from the learners. Within the same session, the instructor can provide feedback and assess the performance of the learners based on their participation in class. Finally, the instructor can ask for suggestions or comments on how they can apply what they had learnt to their work, or generalise what they had learnt to other situations.

A board plan helps the instructor organise the discussion and record the points made by learners so that they can visualise their learning. It is up to the instructor to plan how they would like to organise the discussion using the boards in class. Fig. 9.1 shows a board plan for the teaching plan shown in Table 9.1.

Alternatively, the board plan can also be designed to capture how the instructor chooses to analyse the teaching case (Fig. 9.2).

The call plan is a participation plan where the instructor plans how he/she intends to invite participation for the discussion. The instructor can develop a preference list which identifies learners whom the instructor

Table 9.1 Teaching plan using Events of Learning

Time plan	Instructional design	Actions/activities	Call plan	Overview of the analysis/content covered
2 mins	Gagné Event 1 & 2: 'gain attention' and 'inform learning objectives'	Welcome learners to class with startling new statistics of subject matter. Inform learners the learning outcomes of the course and how it is aligned to the larger programme.	Nil	Learning objectives in the programme outline.
3 mins	Gagné Event 3 & 4: 'stimulate recall of prior learning' and 'present content'	Invite learners to recall prior learning. Present theories, models, concepts, etc. that are associated with the teaching case.	Nil	Subject matter content (e.g. Porter's Five Forces, Value Chain)
5 mins	Gagné Event 5: 'provide learning guidance'	State learning contract of a case method class.	Nil	Establish learning contract (e.g. marks are given for participation, one conversation at a time, no right or wrong answer, etc.).
10 mins	Gagné Event 6: 'elicit performance'	Set the context of the case.	Invite volunteers	Outline the consumer base in context of the country, industry, regulations, etc.
10 mins		Analyse the sector in which the organisation operates. Correspond to discussion questions 1 & 2.	Open to all	Apply SWOT, PEST, Porter's Five Forces or other models to frame the analysis. Highlight the interplay among these areas.

(continued)

Table 9.1 (continued)

Time plan	Instructional design	Actions/activities	Call plan	Overview of the analysis/content covered
20 mins		Ask learners to describe the options available to the organisation, decide on the option that they would choose, and explain their choice. Correspond to discussion questions 3 & 4.	Avoid calling on learners who are employees of the organisation	Consider 3 to 5 options. These should be already outlined in the teaching case plus one option on 'Others'.
10 mins		Provide an epilogue (e.g. Case B) of what happened.	Invite learners who are employees of the organisation to comment	Highlight the key decisions and their outcomes.
10 mins	Gagné Event 7: 'provide feedback'	Wrap up by aligning to conceptual frameworks or models. Re-state learning objectives and provide feedback.	Nil	Discuss and make reference to conceptual models and frameworks.
5 mins	Gagné Event 8 & 9: 'assess performance' and 'enhance retention and transfer to job'	Assess performance of the class and invite learners to reflect on how they will transfer learning. Correspond to discussion question 5.	Cold call, if needed	

Strengths	Weaknesses	Opportunities	Threats

Option A	Option B	Option C	Option D: Others
Reasons:	Reasons:	Reasons:	Reasons:

Fig. 9.1   Board plan design 1

Issues	Alternatives	Recommendations
Analysis	Assumptions	Rationales

Fig. 9.2   Board plan design 2

would like to call on. These are learners who will be given priority if they volunteer at the same time as other volunteers. Usually, this is used for grading purposes as marks are given for class participation.

9.2.2   Learning Cycle

The Honey and Mumford Learning Cycle[6] can also be used to design the teaching plan. The learning cycle starts with 'Having an Experience' where learners experience the case method through individual preparation, small group discussion and large group discussion. Next in the cycle is 'Reviewing the Experience' where learners step back and reflect on the case discussion to draw their own conclusions as a result of the discussions. Using their reflection, learners enter the third part of the learning cycle which is called 'Concluding from the Experience'. Here, learners consolidate their thinking and use theories to explain their conclusions. Finally, the learning cycle ends with 'Planning the Next Steps' where learners plan how they would apply the knowledge that they had gained from this experience to their next assignment or activity. This could culminate into Case B, a new case, or a related assignment in the same programme. A teaching plan can also be constructed using the Honey and Mumford Framework (Table 9.2).

9.2.3   Other Instructional Design Approaches

Instructors can modify and customise their teaching plan to fit their preferred style and method of delivery. Table 9.3 shows another well-used approach which incorporates small group discussions into the large group discussion. However, this is only effective if the class size is around 20 to 25 persons where learners are placed in groups of four or five. If groups are too large, there may not be sufficient opportunities for every learner to contribute their views. Furthermore, if there are too many small groups and every group has to present their findings in turn, it will be challenging to ensure that every learner is sufficiently engaged to sit through all the presentations.

Provide broad questions to guide the groups in their discussion. Provide clear instructions, for example, state clearly if the group should focus on a particular question, or if the group is required to present on certain questions after discussion). During the small group discussions, the instructor helps to clarify doubts or stimulate thinking on certain issues if discussions are not forthcoming.

As the groups present their findings, the instructor would comment, ask for views from other learners, and delve deeper into the three to four issues that are essential to achieving the learning outcomes. Finally, the instructor closes the session by bringing the discussion back to the purpose of the discussion and directs the learners to key takeaways. In addition, you can incorporate a dialogue session or plenary with experts from the organisation or with the protagonist. This gives learners the opportunity to direct their questions to the experts and listen to their views first-hand.

Table 9.2 Teaching plan using Learning Cycle

Time plan	Instructional plan	Actions/activities	Call plan	Overview of the analysis/content covered
		Individual preparation before class		
		Small group discussions before class		
		Large group discussion in class		
10 mins	Having an experience	Set the context of the case.	Invite volunteers.	Outline the consumer base in context of the country, industry, regulations, etc.
10 mins		Analyse the sector in which the organisation operates. Correspond to discussion questions 1 & 2.	Open to all.	Use SWOT, PEST, Porter's Five Forces or other models to frame the analysis. Highlight the interplay among these areas.
20 mins		Ask learners to describe the options available to the organisation, decide on the option that they would choose, and explain their choice. Correspond to discussion questions 3 & 4.	Activate preference call list.	Consider 3 to 5 options. These should be already outlined in the teaching case plus one option on 'Others'.
5 mins	Reviewing the experience	Assess performance of the class and invite learners to reflect on how they will transfer learning.	Invite learners who are employees of the organisation to comment. Cold call other, if needed.	–
10 mins	Concluding from the experience	Invite learners to suggest conceptual models that can frame the insights of the discussion. Instructor can also present content of specific frameworks and theories.		Develop/apply conceptual models and frameworks.
15 mins	Planning the Next Steps	Apply to techniques and insights gained to the discussion of Case B and Case C, or another teaching case in the same programme.		–

Table 9.3   Teaching plan using small group discussions in class

Time plan	Instructional design	Actions/activities	Call plan	Overview of analysis/content covered
5 mins	Inform Learning Outcomes	Introductions and instructions. Set the context of the case.	Nil	–
20 mins	Independent Learning in Small Groups	Small group discussions	Nil	–
30 mins	Elicit Performance	Presentations by each group (2 mins per group). As each group presents, instructor highlights specific areas and invites comments.	Open to all	Group presentations and analyses
15 mins	Q&A with Expert	Invite the protagonist to class for a question and answer session with learners	Open to all	Specific to the organisation and teaching plan
10 mins	Alignment to Concepts	Link to theory or framework	Nil	Explain selected theories, concepts and frameworks
5 mins	Reflection and Transfer	Invite learners to reflect on how they will transfer learning. Wrap up and conclude session.	Open to all	–

9.3   FACILITATED LEARNING

Instructors conduct the case method by facilitating discussions in class. The role of the instructor is to help learners achieve the learning outcome through active listening, facilitating discussion, managing energy level of the class, recording and clarifying information, managing discussion time and mediating disagreements when necessary. Instructors using the case method transfer the ownership of learning to the learners so that they are involved in their own learning. The word 'facilitate' means to make easier. In education, facilitation involves using a collection of classroom methods and strategies to involve learners as much as possible.

Because the ownership of learning resides in the learner, case method classes are best conducted in U-shaped classrooms with sufficient board space. U-shaped classrooms are preferred because these enable learners to focus on the instructor who stands in the centre of the class, as well as for them to have eye contact with their peers when debating and discussing case issues.

9.3.1   Prior to Class

Facilitated learning is choreography meticulously conceptualised and energetically executed by the instructor, with improvisation as he/she interacts with learners. As with any choreography, a lot of time is spent in preparation.

The instructor must know the teaching case exceedingly well. Also, consider how this teaching case fits with the rest of the course, especially in terms of how it relates to previous and subsequent sessions. Discuss the teaching case with the case writer, subject matter experts or with peers who had taught the case previously to learn from their experience on the case.

Choreograph how you would like to lead the class in the discussion. Besides the information provided in the teaching note, prepare and keep handy a list of thought-provoking questions in case you need these to further engage learners. Instructors need to prepare well before they can conduct a good case method class.

9.3.2   *During Class*

When an instructor facilitates the learning experience, he is guided by these two principles:

- Learners had been given valid and relevant information so that they can analyse it independently and make informed choices.
- Learners will take responsibility for the choice and position that they take based on their analysis and judgement.

At the start of the session set ground rules on how you expect the session to be conducted. These could include:

- Respect and value one another's opinion.
- No personal attacks.
- Listen and contribute your views.
- One conversation at a time.
- Give feedback in a constructive manner.

Ensure that the learners understand the learning process, the learning outcomes and the ground rules. Learners should start on equal footing, for example, all should have read the teaching case before attending the case class. If not, provide an overview of the case and highlight the challenges and action that is required by learners.

Obtain views from everyone. To invite more comments, ask thought-provoking questions that are based on the learning outcomes but phrased in such a way that could elicit learner response to address the key issues of the teaching case. Cold call on learners if needed so that everyone's views can be heard.

Although the facilitation process is guided by the teaching note, there may be instances where instructors have to modify their plans depending on class interactions and how discussion evolves. The teaching note is only a guide for the session, instructors must improvise—they need to know when to adjust and adapt. At the end of the session, the instructor consolidates comments, summarises the issues raised and highlights key points of agreement and disagreement.

A good instructor is not one with all the answers but someone who can help learners see different points of view and make their own substantiated decisions on the path to take. Here are some simple rules to remember when facilitating discussion:

- Pace the discussion and keep it moving so that it is neither too fast nor too slow.
- Centre discussion on only one aspect of the case or analysis.
- Bring out the full range of options, alternatives and opinions regarding the issue.
- Craft questions carefully to avoid confusing learners.
- Avoid questions that require insider knowledge.
- Encourage different viewpoints to encourage lively discussion.
- Allow other learners to comment and show alternative views.
- Listen carefully and expand on learners' views.
- Improvise when needed; don't follow teaching plan blindly.
- Move around the room and be close to learners when they speak.
- Make sure that there are no distractions when learners are speaking.
- Prepare to be challenged.
- Refrain from showing off your expertise in the area.
- Allow learners to arrive at the answers themselves.
- Be conscious of body language.
- Gradually wrap up the session meaningfully; avoid abrupt conclusions.

NOTES

1. Smith, M. K. (1996, 2000). 'Curriculum theory and practice'. The Encyclopedia of Informal Education.
2. Gagné, Robert M. (1985). The Conditions of Learning and the Theory of Instruction, (4th ed.), New York: Holt, Rinehart, and Winston.
3. Kolb David. (1984). Experiential Learning: Experience as the Source of Learning and Development. Englewood Cliffs, New Jersey: Prentice Hall.
4. Honey, Peter. & Mumford, Alan. (1982) Manual of Learning Styles London: P Honey.
5. Gagné, Robert M. (1985). The Conditions of Learning and the Theory of Instruction, (4th ed.), New York: Holt, Rinehart, and Winston.
6. Honey, Peter. & Mumford, Alan. (1982) Manual of Learning Styles London: P Honey.

CHAPTER 10

The Teaching Note

That which looks simple and easy is masterful,
requiring much thought and preparation.

Since the case method is a choreographed learning process led by the instructor for inductive learning, all teaching cases have a teaching note to explain how the case can be discussed in class and what are some of the key lessons and reactions the teaching case intends to draw out from the learners. However, the case method is only one of the many instructional methods used for facilitated learning. Case studies can be used in class using other instructional methods of delivery.

A teaching case is not complete until it has been taught. The teaching note is a document that guides instructors how to teach the case study. It is specific to the case study which means that every teaching case should have a teaching note. It is possible for a teaching case to have more than one teaching note especially when the teaching case is used by different instructors for different courses or subjects.

There is a common misconception that that the teaching note should only be written after the teaching case has been completed. Unlike research and knowledge-capture cases where learning occurs independently through reading, the teaching case is written specifically for learning through the case method. The learning outcomes and instructional design of the case method class inform how the case writer ought to conceptualise and compose the teaching case. Simply for this reason, it turns out to

© The Author(s) 2018
J. Gwee, *The Case Writer's Toolkit*,
https://doi.org/10.1007/978-981-10-7173-7_10

be more practical and effective for case writers to either write the teaching note first or write the teaching note and teaching case simultaneously.

The bulk of the teaching note describes in detail the intended design of the large group discussion. It contains a teaching plan which is a blueprint that outlines the design of the large group discussion process. It describes sequence of topics to be discussed, a corresponding time plan for each of these topics, the board plan for the topics and the participation plan (when to invite for volunteers, when to activate a call list, or who to call upon). A time plan is a schedule of when the instructor carries out specific aspects of the teaching activity. Since the teaching note contains pedagogical instructions on how the teaching case is discussed and analysed in class, the teaching note should be based on sound learning theories and educational models (Chap. 9).

There are no templates to what a teaching note ought to look like. It is a set of instructions for the instructor and it should contain information that help the instructor conduct the case method class. To help you compose your teaching note, use these headings as a guide and customise them to the topic of your teaching case.

a. Title of the Teaching Case

The title of the teaching note is the title of the teaching case. If there is a serial number for the teaching case, this is repeated for the teaching note but with the suffix 'TN' added to it (e.g. 2017-01-TN). This will help you keep track of your documents.

b. Synopsis of the Teaching Case

Provide a one paragraph summary of the teaching case to highlight the main issues, key decision points, key decision-maker and organisation, as well as the time and place in which the event in the teaching case is taking place. It also provides an overview of the teaching case. First, the synopsis should mirror the synopsis found in the case study concept plan. Second, and more critical for instructors, is to highlight, upfront, the primary and secondary issues that the teaching case must surface.

c. Learning Outcomes

These are the same learning outcomes outlined in the case study concept plan. Repeat them in the teaching note to align the teaching note to the case study concept plan. This will inform the instructor the purpose of the teaching case and the case session.

d. Name of the Programme

A single teaching case can be used in different programmes or for different runs of the same programme. Identify what these are and describe them if necessary. If there are programme descriptions, you can include them here as well.

e. Target Learner Level and Profile

Indicate the target learners and their profile. The more details you have on the target learners, the better the instructor can contextualise the case method session to their learning needs. The description of target learners could include their background, age, gender, educational qualifications, cultural diversity, language ability and any special needs that they may have.

f. Discussion Questions

List three to five questions for individual and small group discussions here. The discussion questions guide learners how to approach the analysis of the teaching case and steer them in the direction of how the case would be discussed in class. Instructors may or may not ask identical questions in class. Some may choose to stimulate class discussions with parallel or leading questions that tap on learners' prior preparation based on their earlier analyses.

g. Teaching Plan

This is a description of the instructor's action plan to conduct the large group discussion in class. The teaching plan can be based on instructional design theories such as those of Gagné, and Honey and Mumford (Chap. 9). It includes the lesson plan, time plan, board plan and call plan. The teaching strategy is based on the personal preference and teaching style of the instructor, and his/her judgement of how the learning outcomes can best be achieved given the profile of the target audience.

h. Supplementary Materials for Learners

Include additional readings or related materials (e.g. magazine articles, videos, presentation slides) to be assigned to learners to supplement the teaching case. Other forms of learning aids should also be listed here. These are materials given to learners over and above the teaching case and are different from the reference materials given to instructors to enhance their understanding of the teaching case (item j. of same section).

i. Case Analysis

The answers and analyses of the discussion questions, as well as follow-up questions that the instructor will be using in class, are provided here. Arguments for different options, decisions and rationales of choices are outlined in detailed, including technical calculations and financial analysis.

Tables, charts, figures, models, frameworks and so on are also included here, if the instructor intends to highlight these during the discussion in class. The workings and calculation of numbers and financial data are shown here to demonstrate how answers were derived. All answers and data should be interpreted and analysed from the teaching case and not from additional external sources, unless previously specified by the instructor.

Writing the analysis is a check on the sufficiency and relevance of information in the teaching case. Learners should be able to answer the questions based on the information provided in the case study. If they cannot find the necessary information in the teaching case to form their answers, then there are gaps in the case study. The analysis should also achieve the learning outcomes.

j. Additional References

Additional readings should be included in the teaching note to help instructors understand the key issues better. This is particularly helpful for instructors who are not authors of the teaching case. This section can include teaching aids because there may be a variety of ways in which the learning can be enhanced. Teaching aids could include company videos, brochures, advertisements and so on.

k. Feedback

Feedback from instructors who had used the teaching case in different classes are included in this section. Even if the same case study is used to teach the same subject, every class is different with their own set of dynamics. The case experience is enhanced and enriched when instructors share their experience in conducting the teaching case. Comments on what worked or did not work help instructors improve on their teaching strategy and usage of the teaching case.

If the teaching case has been used in other programmes, always document the reactions, comments, inputs and feedback received. The purpose is to give instructors more information about how the teaching case has been received in other sessions with different learners. The feedback can help facilitators improve their case method class. Some helpful feedback may include:

- Be sure to cover the additional readings before starting the case discussion.
- Avoid calling early on someone with experience in this industry.
- The calculations required will challenge most learners.
- Set aside additional time for quantitative analysis.
- For undergraduates, review the immediate and basic issues first.
- For graduates, start directly with the alternatives.
- Start with a vote on the top two alternatives first.
- Identify all possible alternatives before discussing the specific ones.

After piloting the teaching case, instructors and case writers should verify whether the teaching case meets these criteria:

- Could learners achieve the learning outcomes based on the information presented in the teaching case?
- Did the teaching case sufficiently engage and challenge learners and instructors in discussing the issues?

The teaching note may vary with each discussion of the teaching case and has to be reviewed or prepared anew each time. When the same case is used more than once and for different programmes, the discussion questions may change. As a result, the teaching plan and analysis in the teaching note may also change each time the teaching case is taught.

Teaching Note for the Case Study *Charting a New Course*

Part A: Learning Outcomes, Background and Teaching Plan

1. Learning outcomes

- To assess the telecommunications industry and the opportunities and threats that it presents to SingTel Yellow Pages.
- To evaluate the strengths and weakness of SingTel Yellow Pages and the value that the organisation can create.

- To propose new strategies and business model for SingTel Yellow Pages in a deregulated telecommunications industry.

2. Estimated time

75 mins.

3. Target audience

- Undergraduate and postgraduate students
- Students in executive development programmes
- Participants in corporate training programmes

4. Name of programme

- Strategic Management 101
- New Employee Induction Programme

5. Case synopsis

As the trend of privatisation moved into the Asia Pacific in the mid-1990s, many industries had to re-invent themselves. One of the changes was the deregulation of the telecommunications industry. This case study describes the challenges confronted by telephone directory publisher SingTel Yellow Pages. It highlights the opportunities and threats faced by SingTel Yellow Pages, as well as examine the company's strengths and weaknesses. This case study describes the company's key considerations when re-inventing itself.

6. Learner pre-reading

- Case study on *Charting a New Course*
- These discussion questions can be distributed before the class to help students prepare:

  Q1. Analyse the strengths and weaknesses of SingTel Yellow Pages in the context of industry deregulation.

  Q2. Explain the Value Chain of SingTel Yellow Pages and describe how this can help it create sustainable competitive advantage?

Q3. How can SingTel Yellow Pages differentiate? What options does it have to respond and survive in a liberalised market?

7. Additional references

- Ministry of Information and the Arts, Media Division, 'Bring forward full competition in the telecommunications sector', Statement by Mr Yeo Cheow Tong, Minister for Communications and Information Technology at Press Conference on 21 Jan 2000 at 6 pm.
- Loizos Heracleous, 'State ownership, privatization and performance in Singapore: An exploratory study from a management perspective', Asia Pacific Journal of Management, March 2001, Volume 18, Issue 1, pp. 69–81.

8. Teaching Plan

Time plan	Actions/activities	Call plan	Overview of the analysis/content covered
1 min	Inform learners the learning outcomes of the course and how it is aligned to the larger programme.	Nil	Learning outcomes in the programme outline.
1 min	Invite learners to recall prior learning. Present theories, models, concepts, etc., associated with the teaching case.	Nil	Porter's Five Forces and Value Chain
3 mins	State learning contract of a case method class.	Nil	Establish learning contract—marks are given for participation, one conversation at a time, no right or wrong answer.
5 mins	Set the context of the case.	Invite volunteers	Outline the consumer base in context of the country, industry, regulations, etc.
10 mins	Analyse the sector in which the organisation operates. Correspond to Q1.	Open to all	Apply SWOT, PEST, Porter's Five Forces or other models to frame the analysis. Highlight the interplay among these areas.

(continued)

(continued)

Time plan	Actions/activities	Call plan	Overview of the analysis/content covered
10 mins	Analyse the organisation SingTel Yellow Pages. Correspond to Q2.	Open to all	Apply Value Chain.
20 mins	Ask learners to describe the options available to the organisation, decide on the option that they would choose, and explain their choice. Correspond to Q3.	Avoid calling on learners who are employees of the organisation	Consider 3 to 5 options. These should be already outlined in the teaching case plus one option on 'Others'.
10 mins	Provide an epilogue (e.g. Case B) of what happened.	Invite comments.	Highlight the key decisions and their outcomes.
10 mins	Wrap up by aligning to conceptual frameworks or models. Re-state learning objectives and provide feedback.	Nil	Discuss and connect to conceptual models and frameworks.
5 mins	Assess performance of the class and invite learners to reflect on how they will transfer learning.	Cold call, if needed	

Part B: Questions and Possible Answers

This section identifies key ideas arising from the case. These ideas are not intended to be prescribed answers but to help instructors frame their discussions.

Q1: Analyse the strengths and weaknesses of SingTel Yellow Pages in the context of industry face of deregulation.

Strengths

Since 1967, SingTel Yellow Pages had been the official publisher of the Yellow Pages in Singapore. The identity of SingTel Yellow Pages had become linked with that of the Yellow Pages. In other words, SingTel Yellow Pages and Yellow Pages were synonymous to both the industry partners and the general public. This had been a strength of the company because it was able to leverage on an existing brand name. SingTel Yellow Pages was a subsidiary of the telecommunication conglomerate, SingTel Group, which had extensive experience and linkages regionally and internationally. This gave SingTel Yellow Pages many opportunities to expand overseas.

Over the years, SingTel Yellow Pages developed a strong and comprehensive database. Additionally, the infrastructure for printed directories became well-established. SingTel Yellow Pages also gained experience and economies of scale in publishing and distributing its directory products. Most directory companies in the world purchased directory compilation systems from vendors or outsourced distribution to service bureaus. SingTel Yellow Pages, on the other hand, had developed its own directory compilation system which gave the company flexibility and speed when changing from one publication to another. It also allowed the company to support different languages and language applications to meet special requirements.

Weaknesses

The fact that SingTel Yellow Pages and Yellow Pages were synonymous was also the company's Achilles heel. Since Yellow Pages was the main revenue source for the company, a substantial amount of time and resources had also been poured into exploiting this source. With the liberalisation of the telecommunications industry, the company realised that it needed to divert dependence on the Yellow Pages and explore other opportunities. However, developing other products and markets would take at least five to six years before the company could achieve a stable bottomline.

Another weakness was that the company's core competence had been in print publishing. As new technologies emerged and markets shifted, SingTel Yellow Pages was finding it increasingly difficult to grow and look for new and different ways to re-invent itself.

Q2: Explain the Value Chain of SingTel Yellow Pages and describe how this can help it create sustainable competitive advantage?

SingTel Yellow Pages's value chain describes its core competence and competitive advantages. It is shown in this diagram (Fig. 10.1):

	INBOUND LOGISTICS	OPERATIONS	OUTBOUND LOGISTICS	MARKETING & SALES	SERVICES	MARGIN
FIRM INFRASTRUCTURE	Senior management – to provide direction and support for implementation of strategy of pre-empting the competitors through Product Leadership, Operational Excellence and Customer Intimacy. Lobby Telecommunication Authority of Singapore ("TAS") to support strategy.					
HUMAN RESOURCE MANAGEMENT					1. Training on customer service 2. Suggestion and reward system to motivate staff to improve customer service and quality	
TECHNOLOGY DEVELOPMENT	1. Provision of integrated database of subscriber information for TAS – ease of transfer with other telecommunication companies. 2. Printers – print to plate applications integrated with directory compilation system	1. Integration of electronic and print products and/or services allows accuracy and real-time information of integrated database 2. Multi-language platform 3. R&D on electronic products for enhancement	1. System support and application for the Phone book distribution exercise - application to monitor pick-up rates (by subscriber and centres), changes in distribution patterns, directory inventory levels and print quantity.	1. Application for monitoring sales performance by product, individual, group, etc. for sales action. 2. Applications for Market Research and to determining customer needs. 3. Support in product enhancements and development. 4. Tracking mechanism for advertisers.	1. Developments of customer services application to support Call centre applications for customer service – billings, complains, etc. 2. Design of user friendly, multiple and powerful search and quality connecting features that is transparent to users.	
PROCUREMENT	1. Better leverage and negotiation power in collective purchases for all projects – paper and printing.	1. State-of-the-art technology – graphic design and re-production. 2. Ability to use digital advertisements for printing and electronic operations		1. Leverage and use of SingTel umbrella in negotiations of master contract for media placements	–	
	1. Timeliness in paper to printers. 2. Ensuring the smooth and timely transmission of subscriber data from telcos. 3. Minimise printing errors in advertisements 4. Efficient technical support of system and equipment. 5. Timeliness in the delivery of directories to distribution centres 6. Minimise damages directories 7. Establishment of network of suppliers for outsourcing of support works.	1. Faster turnaround – stream line processes, faster turnaround for advertisers 2. Graphic support for print and electronic products	1. Organisation of events for collection of phone books and value offerings of SingTel products. 2. The use of SingTel and SingTel subsidiary facilities as a distribution centres. 3. Distribution to follow customers patterns	1. Bundling of print and electronic products and/or services. 2. Development of new products and/or service 3. Promote on Brand name 4. Create value	1. Differentiate on service and offerings for advertisers – from key to small accounts. 2. Development of a Customer Service and Loyalty program 3. Newsletter for Advertisers 4. Collaboration with SingTel subsidiaries for incentives for customers	MARGIN
	INBOUND LOGISTICS	**OPERATIONS**	**OUTBOUND LOGISTICS**	**MARKETING & SALES**	**SERVICES**	

Fig. 10.1 Value Chain of SingTel Yellow Pages

Even with a value chain, it would be challenging for any company, let along SingTel Yellow Pages, to improve performance in every operational area at the same time. Because resources were finite, strategies had to be developed and implemented within existing constraints. Identifying the right strategy was only one part of the equation to succeed. The other part was having the right people who were committed to SingTel Yellow Pages's transformation. Often, companies start well by rallying employees to its vision but fail to sustain the level of enthusiasm over time.

Q3: How can SingTel Yellow Pages differentiate? What options does it have to respond and survive in a liberalised market?

Using Porter's Generic Strategy, this could be done through cost differentiation, cost focus or differentiation focus. This teaching note proposed differentiation strategy because SingTel Yellow Pages was the market leader then and should continue to build on and strengthen its brand equity and brand instead of concentrating all it resources to reduce cost. Reduction of cost would not guarantee that SingTel Yellow Pages directories and services would be preferred by the customers since it would only be a matter of time before new entrants also reap and benefit from the economies of scale and experience. To differentiate, SingTel Yellow Pages could consider product leadership, operational excellence and customer intimacy.

Product Leadership
To fortify its position as the only competent publisher and market leader of the directory market, SingTel Yellow Pages could leverage users' and advertisers' preferences and dependence on SingTel Yellow Pages directories. Either groups would incur switching costs should they choose to migrate to other sources for similar services. To position SingTel Yellow Pages's directories as the prime, national information products and reference tool, it would need to enhance existing products and develop and introduce new ones. Some possibilities are:

- Colour advertisement on white newsprint as opposed to conventional black over yellow newsprint. Colour would attract readers' attention and focus their line of vision.
- 'Front-of-book' enhancements to break the monotony of classifications and listings.
- Bilingual listings for countries and markets that had more than one language of communication for commerce.
- Incorporate URLs and domain addresses to complement the fast adoption of information technology.

Operational Excellence

SingTel Yellow Pages had already established a firm and efficient infrastructure, and amassed considerable experience and economies of scale in publishing and distributing its directory products. With new entrants to the market, SingTel Yellow Pages had to innovate by tapping on information and new technologies to improve internal processes and cycle time. It must also reduce cost and wastage, support the development of new products and services, decrease error rates and rejections and so on.

Customer Intimacy

Given its established track record, SingTel Yellow Pages must find new ways to exceed the perceived value of its products and services. At this point, learners can be invited to propose way in which this can be done.

Conceptual Models

The conceptual models and frameworks that will be used in the discussion are the Value Chain[1] and Five Forces.[2]

Conclusion and Final Remarks

At the end of the session, these are some of the key takeaways that the instructor can highlight to the class:

1. In order for SingTel Yellow Pages to succeed in its strategy, it has to seize opportunities and then prioritise its options for both short-term and long-term gains.

2. The board of director, management and staff must be committed to the changes. They must move as a whole in the agreed direction.
3. SingTel Yellow Pages must align to the objectives of its parent company, SingTel, so that it can continue to leverage on the opportunities provided through this association.
4. SingTel Yellow Pages must identify core competencies that are sustainable and non-imitable.
5. The Value Chain analysis is a good tool to understand organisations.
6. The Three Generic Strategies model can help organisations plan and prioritise its strategies.

Participants are invited to give feedback and reactions to the session that they have just participated in.

Instructor can also inform learners of the subsequent developments of SingTel Yellow Pages:

In 2003, SingTel divested SingTel Yellow Pages Pte Ltd. Yellow Pages (Singapore) Pte Ltd, a company equally owned by JP Morgan Partners Asia and CVC Asia Pacific, acquired certain businesses, assets and liabilities of SingTel Yellow Pages Pte Ltd at S$220 million. Six months later, Yellow Pages (Singapore) Pte Ltd was listed on SGX-ST.

In 2009, the company changed its name to Global Yellow Pages Limited. The following year, in September 2010, Global Yellow Pages Limited partnered with StarHub, an integrated information provider, to offer bundled services for small medium-sized enterprises.

On August 1, 2017, Global Yellow Pages announced that it would restructure to focus on real estate as its core business and cease publication of print directories (i.e. Yellow Pages, Yellow and White Pages Chinese, and White Pages Business Listings) from 2018. The digital products of Yellow Pages would operate under a new company, Yellow Pages Pte Ltd (YP), and print-advertisers could shift to online platforms. Global Yellow Pages would have 20% stake in YP.

NOTES

1. Michael E. Porter, *Competitive Advantage: Creating and Sustaining Superior Performance*, Free Press, January 1985.
2. Michael E. Porter, *Competitive Strategy: Techniques for Analysing Industries and Competition*, Free Press, June 1998.

Index[1]

---

[1] Note: Page numbers followed by 'n' refer to notes.

© The Author(s) 2018
J. Gwee, *The Case Writer's Toolkit*,
https://doi.org/10.1007/978-981-10-7173-7